ONCE IRON GIRLS

ONCE IRON GIRLS

Essays on Gender by Post–Mao Chinese Literary Women

Translated and Edited
with an Introduction by
HUI WU

LEXINGTON BOOKS
A division of

ROWMAN & LITTLEFIELD PUBLISHERS, INC.
Lanham • Boulder • New York • Toronto • Plymouth, UK

Published by Lexington Books
A division of Rowman & Littlefield Publishers, Inc.
A wholly owned subsidary of The Rowman & Littlefield Publishing Group, Inc.
4501 Forbes Boulevard, Suite 200, Lanham, Maryland 20706
http://www.lexingtonbooks.com

Estover Road, Plymouth PL6 7PY, United Kingdom

British Library Cataloguing in Publication Information Available

Library of Congress Cataloging-in-Publication Data

The hardback edition of this book was previously cataloged by the Library of
Congress as follows:

Essays on gender by post-Mao Chinese literary women / Hui Wu.
    p. cm.
  Includes bibliographical references and index.
  1. Chinese literature—20th century—History and criticism. 2. Chinese
literature—20th century—Women authors. 3. Gender identity—China.
4. China—Intellectual life—1976– I. Wu, Hui, 1963–
  PL2308.5.W65E87 2010
  895.1'0992870904—dc22   2009037696

ISBN: 978-0-7391-3421-4 (cloth : alk. paper)
ISBN: 978-0-7391-3422-1 (pbk. : alk. paper)
ISBN: 978-0-7391-3423-8 (electronic)

∞™ The paper used in this publication meets the minimum requirements of
American National Standard for Information Sciences—Permanence of Paper for
Printed Library Materials, ANSI/NISO Z39.48-1992. Printed in the United States
of America

To Tong Donna Chen,
Who continues to be a woman in the true sense of the word

CONTENTS

ACKNOWLEDGMENTS

I must express my gratitude to all who have helped me in one way or another. I am indebted deeply to Daoming Chen, my dear husband, for offering wisdom and hugs whenever I need them; to T. Donna Chen, my beloved daughter, for reading the book in its infancy; to the University Research Council at the University of Central Arkansas for a travel grant and several summer research stipends that enabled me to complete the field work in China and the manuscript; to Professor Marcy Tucker at Texas A&M University at Kingsville, for critiquing the manuscript and offering her insight; and to the Lexington Books editor, Michael Sisskin, for his assistance and appreciation of Chinese literary feminism. And all my other colleagues—Professor Roger Ames at the University of Hawaii, Professor Patricia Bizzell at the College of the Holy Cross, Professors Cheryl Glenn and Xiaoye You at the Penn State University, and anonymous reviewers of my manuscript, are aware of my appreciation of their recommendations of and interest in this book.

Special thank-you notes go to Professor C. Jan Swearingen at Texas A&M University for her long-term friendship and persistent support, Professor Emeritus Winifred B. Horner, and Professor Linda Hughes. Dr. Horner's courses aroused my passion for comparative studies of rhetoric. Dr. Hughes's remark that "One must have freedom to quest" is my inspiration of all time.

Without these people's support and inspiration, I could not have brought Chinese literary women's feminist philosophy and rhetoric to this side of the Pacific. Thank you.

TRANSLATOR'S NOTE

This presentation of post-Mao Chinese literary women's essays on gender is an attempt to provide resources for both specialists and nonspecialists in the study of Chinese women and their writing, including Anglophone teachers and students who may approach Chinese essays for the first time. This opening note explains my selection of the essays and to forestall potential misassumptions about what post-Mao women's essays may offer.

After exhaustive field research, I tried to collect essays by contacting as many writers as I could. Each of the writers in this collection is critically acclaimed in China and in the West alike as a representative figure of contemporary women's literature. Each has some of her works translated into English or critiqued in secondary English sources, with the exception of Han Xiaohui. If some well-known post-Mao women writers—such as Wang Anyi, Tie Ni, or Zhang Xinxing—do not appear in this book, this is because they did not respond to my requests or had not written essays on gender by the time I finished my research.

Studying Chinese women requires an understanding of woman naming, as the writers alternate some names strategically for rhetorical purposes in their essays. First, *nüren* (a female person) often denotes qualities traditionally conceived of as befitting women, such as sweetness, submissiveness, sentimentality, frailty, beauty, and so on. Second, *nüxing* (the female gender) is often used when referring to career women or used as an adjective to appropriate a thought, profession, writing, or culture regarding women. Third, *funü*, an official label adopted in the early 1950s, refers to the collectivity of women working for the state. It is a theoretical term that the state, institutions, organizations, media, and social science have developed to discuss matters concerning women. Tani Barlow calls *funü* a "Confucianized, late imperial, collective compound" (*Questions of Women* 56), which women seldom use to refer to themselves or female individuals (cf. Barlow "Politics and Protocols of *funü*"). Likewise, few writers in this anthology use *funü* to discuss women's daily lives. Almost all of them purposefully choose *nüren*, the term that carries a history of belittling females, to challenge the traditional definition of woman and expected gender roles. They use *nüxing* to refer to women's thoughts, intellect, and writing.

When approaching these essays, the reader should be sensitive to the political conditions under which post-Mao women write about gender inequality. One may notice that not a single writer openly criticizes China's policies. Even if they express criticism of this nature, they do so subtly, evasively, and cautiously. This is because it is politically dangerous to criticize the government openly and directly. The writers are aware of the censorship that might destroy their lives and careers in the name of "stabilizing the state," an excuse to suppress dissidents. Their fragile balance between hope and hopelessness shows how complicated and politically sensitive it is to write essays on gender. Indeed, it is not realistic to call for radical changes within the extant political system. Perhaps their strategy is to modify the gender power structure by gradually transforming the public and women themselves.

While I have defined the Chinese essay and briefly recounted its rhetorical tradition in the "Introduction," I would like to add some notes in terms of its structure and paragraph development. Due to a different rhetorical tradition, Chinese essayists focus on personal, innovative approaches to language and thoughts, depending on the internal contour and not so much on a set of structural forms controlled by the thesis. They anticipate the reader's participation in making the meaning and logical connections. To the Chinese, reading is a serious endeavor that requires cooperation on the reader's part. As Han Xiaohui says, "a learned person only writes for those who can see the meaning," implying that the relationship between a writer and a reader is built on their shared rhetorical assumptions. For this reason, these essays may not meet an English reader's expectation of chain-like logical reasoning typical of the Western essay. This awareness also applies to reading paragraphs in that consistency and division depend on the mood and the tone rather than merely on the point. In order to preserve the original textuality, I have kept most of the ellipses ending sentences or paragraphs, although I am aware of differences in Western composition conventions. I have added occasional transitions, but only when absolutely necessary, to maintain the flow.

It is also important to note that I have provided all the notes and references that may be to the reader's interest. For readers who may want to trace the development of the writers' thoughts, I have provided the publication information as well as the dates of manuscripts whenever available. To remain consistent with the existing literature and show readers where they can find these sources, I have indicated all the quotations previously translated into English with the exception of the ones I translated myself. It is worth explaining that the Chinese believe that citations mar textuality, particularly that of the essay. Thus, an absence of citations does not discredit the essays. Even academic papers were not required to document sources until near the end of the twentieth century, and only under the influence of American academic writing. Therefore, essayists do not provide citations, period. We must trust that the writers have incorporated quotations to the best of their knowledge.

I remind readers that all the women presented are established literary writers. Their styles, sometimes formal and sometimes informal, are elevated and poetic. They play with the word with confidence to create the mood and tone with musicality, the prime requirement for approval in the Chinese essay. I, the translator, have conceived it my duty to adhere faithfully to what the writers mean and to maintain the mood and tone they create. Based on my experiences, I hold an eclectic view of translation between the antithesis that Stephen Owen discusses in *An Anthology of Chinese Literature* that faithful translation means adapting the material to the conventions of the target language and adhering to preserving the difference of the original. I believe, however, in reinventing similar rhetorical effects in the host language without changing the meaning of the original and without compromising readability. Put differently, the translator must put herself in the audience's shoes to feel the effect and draw a fine line between keeping the original tone and mood and rendering them idiomatic and natural in the target language.

According to this principle, I have avoided all paraphrasing not required by language differences to provide translations that are exact and complete in meaning. Depending on the context, I have tried to "English" some terms previously translated. For example, *tian* has been conventionally translated into "heaven," and *qianwan* into "thousands" in other works. I have, instead, chosen "nature" and "countless" to focus on the meaning. I have also condensed some texts to achieve conciseness and simplicity, a desirable quality in the Western essay. Practically all the modifications have been made with writers' permission, and in no case do the changes involve censorship or any intentional alteration.

It should be acknowledged that all translations derive from interpretations of the original. The meaning I think I have faithfully rendered only represents my interpretation. Unavoidably, errors may appear, and for them I am solely responsible.

INTRODUCTION

Hui Wu

In China, it is declared, and even believed, that today's Chinese women are half the sky and as equal as men. Indeed, judged by their public and domestic contributions, women are more than half the sky. However, they are still kept in a position subordinate to men. My personal story serves as an example. As an associate chair of the foreign language department in a Chinese university, I was ordered by one of my male colleagues, the chair, to clean up his desk and office. When asked why, he simply said, "This is a woman's job." If women holding chair positions may indicate gender equality, the fact that I was one of the only two women holding the position of "associate chair" among forty-some departmental heads shows a different picture. It seemed, at least during the time of my service (1987–1993), that most women were qualified merely for an associate or vice position. Only women who have this kind of experience can feel profound sexual discrimination in their daily lives.

As a post-Mao woman who grew up in the Mao era, I share similar life experiences with the writers in this anthology. Growing up under Mao Zedong's rulership (1949–1976), we have been "iron girls" who have done whatever men do in all walks of life—heavy physical labor on the farm or in factories, truck driving, construction work, military training, professional work, or academic work. You name it, we have done it. However, we are constantly told, explicitly and implicitly in various forms, to keep ourselves within "limits" (cf. Ai). Gender inequality shared between post-Mao female writers and myself is the driving force behind this anthology.

All the essays in this book were previously published in newspapers, magazines, periodicals, or anthologies, shedding light on post-Mao women's purposes in fiction writing and their thoughts on gender politics. Each writer is critically acclaimed for her fiction, poetry, or essays. All of them

1

were once passionate believers of the Maoist women's liberation, dissociating themselves with centuries-long gender ideology only to find that they were still sexually unequal in many aspects of life. Due to their unique sociopolitical experiences, post-Mao women may hold gender perspectives different from those of their Western counterparts and other generations in China in their critical inquiries of gender. Indeed, the essays express the views of a particular generation of literary women whose lives and works find no parallels in the West or China.

Each essay expresses the writer's sentiments toward the basic lack of equality and discusses, specifically and in detail, the material reality wherein women live and function. For this reason, my primary task is to present these essays as they are, including alternative gender perspectives that may raise the eyebrows of the Western reader. For example, while criticizing patriarchy and male dominance apparently from a feminist perspective, Han Xiaohui, Lu Xing'er, and Shu Ting claim that "I am not a feminist." Yet readers find strong feminist views in their writing. It is exactly because of their disavowals that I have collected their essays on gender; this contradiction is, I argue, significant in understanding and complicating the various ways we define "feminism."

Feminism, a borrowed Western term, bears layers of historical and cultural connotations to post-Mao women. First, in the early twentieth century, feminism was translated into *nüquan zhuyi* (literally meaning "female-power/right-ism"), which was changed to *nüxing zhuyi* ("femininity," or female gender-ism) in the 1980s. The former reminds Chinese women of the suffrage rhetoric in early twentieth-century China and earlier Western feminism, which is believed to be incompatible with contemporary Chinese women's life experience. First, under Mao, neither men nor women were allowed to vote and to enjoy human rights (*quan*). In the sense of human rights, neither sex had privilege. Therefore, Chinese women's criticism of sexual inequality cannot be narrowly examined with the gender binary of male versus female because "what is often assumed to be the central transaction between women and culture—women's heterosexual relation to men has little relevance to the China crisis" (Chow 83). Second, unlike their Western counterparts, Chinese women did not need to win suffrage (*quan*) under Mao. Without fight, women have been granted the same rights (*quan*) to work and to receive education along with men. Third, post-Mao women writers may feel, not without limitation, that *nüquan zhuyi*, or Western feminism, in promoting gender equality, also promotes gender *sameness*, a rhetoric they feel similar to that of Maoist women's liberation that denies women of womanhood and sexual identity, which these writers believe is an essential part of the humanity.

Nüxing zhuyi, on the other hand, emphasizes gender difference, which Chinese women writers feel downplays women's intellectuality and capability through an emphasis of femininity that society always uses to oppress women. They recognize that male supremacy reflects the traditional and stereotypic view of women's roles as the mother, wife, or daughter—roles that men want women to play for them and roles that largely stop women from developing themselves intellectually and professionally. Singling women out as *nüxing* (the female gender) implies that the female sex is not only different from but also inferior to the male sex, particularly when intellect and profession are concerned. Post-Mao women writers feel that they should be regarded as human first and foremost and then as women when their writing is being judged. They believe that their work is as equally good as men's, and they do not need "-ism" to help them. The purpose of their writing is not to form -isms but to create art work just as men do. Even without affiliation with any "-ism," they still write to educate men and emancipate women from the mentality of the "inferior" sex. For these reasons, post-Mao women writers find it hard to have their names associated with either *nüquan zhuyi* or *nüxing zhuyi* (cf. L. Liu 151).

On the other hand, post-Mao women's perspectives on gender indeed reflect the influence of early Western feminism, despite their ambivalence toward feminism and their recognition that women's material environment under Mao may not be sufficiently explained entirely by theoretical models derived from the experience of Western women (L. Liu 23; Wang Zheng "Maoism, Feminism" 136, "Three Interviews" 165, 193–94; Wu "Alternative" 229–30). In the 1990s, Chinese translations of Western feminist writing, such as Beauvoir's *The Second Sex* and Virginia Wolfe's *A Room of One's Own*, became available. For their own essays, they borrow terms and titles from these translations, even though they are aware that "feminism" (*nüquan zhuyi*) indicates a historical and cultural context different from their own.

Leading Chinese literary progress, post-Mao women writers are urban legends and have developed new styles, genres, and themes in response to social, economic, and political changes since the early 1980s. Despite the changes, they have never deviated from their original goal—a literature by women, of women, and for women. This is in its essence a feminist goal. It is, therefore, compelling to translate these essays for Anglophone readers, who can develop an understanding of post-Mao women writers' standpoints by experiencing the similarities and differences of global feminisms. To this end, this "Introduction" assists the reader with a historical account of post-Mao women's life and literature and their transformation of a male-dominated genre—the essay.

THE LIFE AND LITERATURE OF POST-MAO WOMEN

Debuting in the 1970s, post-Mao Chinese writers are largely known in China as *zhiqing zuojia* (writers of educated youth generation) or *wenge hou zuojia* (post–Cultural Revolution writers), who grew up under Mao (1949–1976) and were forced to abandon middle school, high school, or college education to serve as farmers, factory workers, or soldiers during the Cultural Revolution (1966–1976). Although many Western critics consider them contemporaries of younger generations of writers who came of age in the 1990s, post-Mao women writers' perspectives on gender and their writing agenda are largely different because of their lived experiences under Mao. Younger writers, who did not experience the Cultural Revolution and emerged in the later years of Deng Xiaoping's era of economic reforms, are not identified with *zhiqing zuojia*, or *wengehou zuojia*, a title that embodies a life experience only the post-Mao generation has.

Post-Mao women's life under Mao is paradoxical, complicating feminist theory and criticism of women's literature. In the early 1950s, when they were babies or even before they were born, gender equality was written into the constitution to protect marriages of free will, to outlaw concubinage and child marriage, and to ensure equal pay for equal work. Throughout their lives, they have been told that "women are the same as men" and that "women can do whatever men can do." Women had the equal right to receive formal education and participated in socialist construction to hold "half the sky." Ironically, it was exactly the promotion of gender similarity that denied women "the very language in which to express the gender inequality in their daily lives" (Hershatter 44).

Mao's movement indeed has liberated women in the sense that they have gained strong confidence in intellect, professional development, academic performance, and leadership. Since 1977, the year after Mao's death, when universities began admissions again based on college entrance test scores, college-educated post-Mao women have found out that they are not only as intellectually capable as men but in many ways, better, smarter, and more competent because they are able to juggle a full-time job and the full load of housework. They are also decision-makers in terms of family finances, children's education, and relationships with relatives. As academics and professionals, they are fully capable of meeting challenges in math and science. Women doctors and scientists are normal phenomena. The one-child policy does not allow them a second birth, and with support from their parents or in-laws, it also allows them to end reproduction and focus on career afterward.[1] Women in post-Mao era challenge the portrayal of China as the home of an entrenched patriarchal family system.

On the other hand, post-Mao women's lives challenge the perception of China as a society where Mao's movement has liberated women from the patriarchal system. Not surprisingly, the impact of Mao's liberation of women remains a controversy among researchers. Many scholars recognize that the Maoist women's liberation has, to a large degree, overthrown traditional gender ideology and fully placed women in society (Zhong, Wang, and Bai). Wang Zheng believes that "the CCP [Chinese Communist Party]-created presumption that 'Chinese women were liberated' was a fact beyond questioning" ("Research" 2). However, the investigations of Elizabeth Croll (*Changing Identities*), Mingxia Chen, and Yu Xiong demonstrate disparities between the images of equality and the daily reality of inequality. Gail Hershatter concludes, "Women's domestic labor was rendered invisible, and time spent performing it made women less able to rise to supervisory positions" (44). Li Xiaojiang, a leading Chinese feminist critic, and others argue that Mao's liberation of women was mainly to mobilize them as a labor force for national goals, for it held male standards as the norm and required women to meet men's criteria (Li; Stacey 238–39; Hershatter 44; Wu). Chinese women are liberated legally and theoretically, but deep down, within the family and institutions, traditional gender ideology still prevails.

The primary purpose of Mao's liberation of women is to increase industrial and agricultural production. Accordingly, gender equality meant mobilizing women to join men for Mao's revolution (Stacey 238–39). The rhetoric of "answering the Party's calls" and "going to where Chairman Mao directs" deepened the political and physical exploitation of women. Women seemed liberated by joining men in the public sphere, yet they were required to satisfy the double demands from both the state and the family. Mao declared, "In order to build a great socialist society it is most important to mobilize the masses of women to join in productive activity" (23). Involved defenselessly in heavy physical labor under primitive, even toxic and life-threatening, conditions, Chinese women worked along with men without physical and physiological differences to meet the demands from the state (cf. Honig and Hershatter 4; Jiang 211).

While women undertook nontraditional tasks in the workplace, they were also expected to take care of all housework to support their men's careers. In other words, while a woman could be recognized in public as equal to men, at home she was taken for granted as a wife, daughter, or mother subordinate to male members' needs and careers. The state, while encouraging women to work as men outside the home, also promoted the Confucian ideology to tie women to wifely duties to support their husbands' careers. The double requirements placed a double physical burden on women. Li Xiaojiang points out that "[m]ore than forty years of mental and physical exhaustion" made Chinese women endure a heavy burden that "neither women in history nor contemporary men have experienced!" (374). Chinese women were living "the life of beasts" (Li 376). The double requirements taken for granted by society also subordinate women as the inferior sex in the workplace and at home, consequently reinforcing the patriarchal ideology that "men are superior and women are inferior" (*nanzun nübei*).

In practice, the rhetoric of "being the same as men" resulted in a chain of negative consequences to women, who were encouraged to follow men as the model. Since Mao's primary goal in liberating women was to use them as a labor force, it legitimized de-sexing women to assimilate them into the male world; yet at the same time, male standards remained dominant and the norm, and in turn, justified the use of male standards to judge women (Min 196; L. Liu 35). Accordingly, a woman had to lose her sexual identity to achieve gender equality. Womanhood was thus deemed inferior to manhood and represented lesser human traits that ought to be suppressed. During the Cultural Revolution, female dignity plummeted to its nadir in history. Femininity was criticized as "pétit bourgeois." Female-specific apparels were condemned as symbols of bourgeois lifestyle. It was a life risk for women to wear makeup, high-heels, and dresses/skirts, or even to keep long hair because all these were seen as corruptive of the Maoist revolutionary spirit. Love, beauty, emotion, courtship, gender relations, sexuality, and family life were privatized and thus forbidden to be discussed publicly. For example, though the Marriage Law protected marriages of personal choice, couples who wanted to be married had to obtain the endorsement from their institutes. Arranged marriages for both sexes by parents or bosses of workplaces were mostly taken for granted privately and officially, but dating out of free choice was mostly kept as a secret until marriage was in the plan. A single woman in her late twenties or a divorced woman was often harassed by gossips and suffered from unfair institutional treatment. Many women were married out of family obligation or social pressure. Moreover, many married women who gave birth to girls suffered from family prejudice. But these problems were not allowed to be discussed publicly, because they were regarded as *women's problems*, private matters that did not deserve public attention. For more than four decades, Chinese women lived supposedly "without sexual identity and differences" (Wang 166). For such a long time, "woman" as a human concept virtually did not exist in China.[2] As far as body politics go, Mao's transformation of women into semi-men, or men "wannabes," deprived women of their human rights and derogated womanhood.

Not until near the end of the 1970s, when the Cultural Revolution came to an end after the death of Mao and the arrest of "the Gang of Four" (a Party faction headed by Mao's third wife, Jiang Qing), did Chinese people see a loosening of the ideological rein. In the early 1980s, China began an economic reform, which revived a tremendous interest in Western science and technology, ideology, individualism, and humanism as well as Western fashion, entertainment, and art forms. Translations of early Western feminist works also became available. The contact with cultures beyond China disillusioned post-Mao women, who realized that the Maoist revolution deprived not only all the Chinese of human rights but also women of their rights to be women. Under Mao, they lost womanhood and the most precious years of their lives when they should have received a formal education.

The inspiration from Western humanism awakened women's gender consciousness. Starting in the late 1970s, post-Mao literary women, led by the majority of those included in this book, initiated a women's movement with fiction and poetry, a movement no longer enveloped in any political campaigns launched by males, such as the New Women Movement in the early twentieth century or women's liberation regulated by Mao (Fan; T. Lu). These women writers made their strong, eagerly awaited debut. Presenting female characters interactive with real life situations in a distinct voice, their literary works focus on the right to seek romantic love and to be women, which is not the end but the means to free women from the political control of the state. Expressed in their texts were strong desires to regain women's human dignity devalued and lost during the Cultural Revolution. For example, Zhang Kangkang's novella, "The Right to Love," expresses strong resentment toward the suppression of women's desires and emotions. Hu Xin's "Four Women of Forty" describes women's anger at institutionalized gender inequality. In Lu Xing'er's "The Sun is Not Out Today," a group of women share anguish and insecurity, while waiting for mandatory abortions in a women's hospital. Shu Ting's poem "Ode to the Oak Tree" expresses women's desires for romantic love on an equal and independent basis. Vividly detailing the pains that have scarred women's lives, the literary works by these and other post-Mao women—such as Chen Rong, Cheng Naishan, Wang Anyi, Zhang Jie, and Zhang Xinxing—exercised phenomenal influence on society and helped women realize that Mao's "gender equality" deprived women of human rights by belittling female integrity.

Meanwhile, the economic reform and free market have also brought Western capitalist practices and commercialization to the fore. The female body, after regaining its femininity, is vastly abused for economic and ideological purposes. The tension between the role of liberated women and the traditional role of the daughter, wife, or mother resurfaces with new problems and dilemmas. While under Mao, urban women were required to leave home and work for socialist construction, now a majority of them are the first group to be laid off under the readjusted economic policy, particularly those over thirty-five. Moreover, it is harder for female college graduates than for their male counterparts to secure professional jobs, because they are around the age when a woman is expected to be married and start a family. At job fairs, some companies even openly announce "No Interviews for Female Applicants." The state policy that a female employee is entitled to a thirty-day maternal leave with pay after giving birth works against women, because businesses simply refuse to hire them to avoid the liability.[3]

Marriage, conventionally perceived as their main life component, imposes extra restraints on women. A woman without a decent job is contemptible to the extent that no man would take her as a wife. On the other hand, a woman with an advanced degree and career success finds it difficult to establish a family as well, because many men reject these "superwomen" (*nü qiangren*) as wives. Although the pressure on single women for marriage has slightly decreased since the 1990s, a woman in her twenties is still pressured to marry, or she is not a woman (*nüren*).[4] It is not unusual that a single woman in her late twenties is subject to sexual harassment or institutional discrimination. Ironically, a married woman may also find herself in a hopeless situation, exhausted due to the double burden or abandoned when her husband has achieved success or when there are conflicts between her career and family. She who succeeds in her career is frequently reminded of her motherly or wifely duties. Oftentimes, this tension forces a woman to compromise her ambitions in order to be accepted as *nüren* by the family and society.

At home, a deep-rooted traditional institution, a woman has little control over her life. Chinese tradition holds that the family is the foundation of the country, and the Chinese characters for "country" or "state" is *guo jia* (state and family in one). To make the country strong, the family must be well regulated. Without officially recognizing it, the state rigorously observes the Confucian doctrine on the relationship among the individual, the family, and the government, which states: "The ancients who wished clearly to exemplify illustrious virtue throughout the world would first set up good government in their states. Wishing to govern their states well, they would first regulate their families. Wishing to cultivate their persons, they would first rectify their minds" (quoted in Y. Lin 129). Family is traditionally a women's domain, where they are considered important, yet subordinate, to their husbands' achievements. The famous modern song "The Mid-Autumn Moon" (*shiwu de yueliang*) repeatedly echoes the centuries-old commandment that "the husband's success honors the wife" (*fugui furong*). The promotion of the "Family of Five Merits" (*wuhao jiating*), or the model family, encourages a woman to sacrifice herself for her parents, her in-laws, her child, her husband, her workplace, and the state. All of the propaganda uses the label of "liberated woman" to confine her to the position subordinate to her husband and the family.

The new problems in the age of economic reforms give incentives to literary women. In the wake of change, they respond to a painfully renewed and evolving gender awareness. While their fiction and poetry in the 1980s stressed the right to love and to regain femininity without polarizing gender relations, their writing in the 1990s criticizes gender inequality at home and in society. Accordingly, repositioning women in public and at home becomes the main theme. The thematic change has opened an unexplored path for post-Mao literary women, and a milestone in women's writing, the female essay (*nüxing sanwen*), has emerged.

REGENDERING THE CHINESE ESSAY

Similar to the Western tradition, Chinese women have no history of essay writing parallel to that of their male counterparts. The classical prose, the original form of the Chinese essay, was started by men and remained predominantly a male domain for centuries. Whenever the "essay" is under discussion, it is male writers—Lu Xun, Zhu Ziqing, Liang Qichao, Yutang Lin, Yang Su, and Hu Shih—that a learned person must never fail to refer to. The classical prose in the Tang (618–907) and Song (960–1127) dynasties has been celebrated, imitated, studied, and analyzed by literary gentry as well as by critics and students in China and in the West alike. In the May Fourth period (1920s–1930s), or the New Cultural Movement,[5] the classical prose developed into the modern essay (*sanwen*), embracing poetic features of the composition of its forefather (cf. Pollard xi).

Mostly short, *sanwen* stands for almost all nonmetric prose but fiction, poetry, drama, and scholarly writing (cf. Pollard xi), including expressive prose (*shuqing sanwen*), narrative prose (*xushi sanwen*), occasional jottings (*suibi*), critical prose (*zawen*), travel writing (*youji*), biographies, brief comments (*xiao pingwen*), prefaces, and letters (Pollard xi; Ma and An 69–70). Demanding high skills and creative power, the Chinese essay is personal, truthful, poetic, expressive, and metaphoric. It is a genre of free choice of theme and style. Conforming to no obvious pattern, its structural unity is governed by the internal requirements of mood, tone, and purpose. The core value of the Chinese essay lies in the freedom it grants to the writer to speak his/her mind, a mind liberated from any rules and conventions to extend the meanings of small matters to big issues.

The freedom of the genre has enabled men to enjoy a long glorious history of power and legacy. To a woman, however, the essay is perhaps the most prohibitive genre—not because it requires high language skills, but because it is closely intertwined with gender politics. First, the classical prose came of age as the vehicle of moral generalization for the purpose of directing personal and social conduct (S. Liu 9). For centuries, the political stage was exclusively men's, so women had no role to play in essay writing. Second, the essay requires the writer to tell the truth and reveal true feelings when making personal connections to public issues (Xie 285). This feature makes it almost impossible to write essays when the ruling authorities tighten political and ideological controls. Unfortunately, China has been often engulfed in ideological purges since the 1942 Yan'an Rectification Campaign (*Yan'an zhengfeng yundong*), wherein all writers were required to make confessions. The same year, Mao delivered two speeches on literary criteria, "Reform in Learning, the Party, and Literature" and "Against Party Stereotype-Writing," which set the political tone for literary creation and criticism—literature must serve the needs of the Party.

Admittedly, writers of both sexes have endured censorship, but female writers face more difficulties because they tend to write about women's problems, topics that were often criticized as self-indulgent, expressive of petit bourgeois sentiments, and counterrevolutionary, because they "distracted" the public from the agenda of the Party. For example, in "Thoughts on March 8," Ding Ling, a renowned female writer of the May Fourth generation, pointed out that the stratification within the Party caused peculiar problems for women (Barlow and Bjorge 316–21). Her writing, however, did not glorify Mao's orthodoxy that required writers to demonstrate their solidarity with the masses and make revolutionary statements. Ding Ling became the target of political criticism in the Yan'an Campaign. Because of her criticism of the problems existing within the Party in that essay, she was persecuted again during the Anti-Rightist Campaign (1957–1958) and was purged out of the Party until the end of the Cultural Revolution (cf. McDougall and Louie 196; Buffton 40). Since the Yan'an period, women's essays on women's lives have been frequently sneered at as "moaning and groaning without illness" (*wubin shenyin*). Put differently, women's issues were privatized and, accordingly, considered too trivial to merit the public's attention.[6] As Amy Dooling and Kristina Torgeson write, "women writers are frequently criticized for focusing narrowly on women's subjects, in particular their own emotional experiences" (26). Consequently, women's essays are considered as inferior as their gender.

During the forty years of Mao's governance, essays expressing writers' true feelings and thoughts hardly existed, except for those celebrating Mao's achievements and the communist revolutionary spirit. The Chinese language textbook, when teaching the genre of essay, only presented those meeting Mao's literary criteria, such as Wei Wei's "Who Is the Most Beloved?" (*shui shi zui keai de ren*) and Yuan Ying's "Ode to the Green Bamboo on the Jinggang Mountains." The former is an ode to the People's Liberation Army during the Korean War in the early 1950s, and the latter a reminiscence of Mao Zedong, who led the "Red Army" to fight nationalists headed by Chiang Kaishek. After the Cultural Revolution, the publication of five volumes of essays, *A Collection of Reflections* (*Suixiang lu*), by Ba Jin, renowned male novelist since the May Fourth period, revitalized the reading public's interest in the essay. Ba Jin was the first to tell truths about political persecutions during the Cultural Revolution. Afterward, many publishers exhumed the essays published in the May Fourth era and began to publish essays on women, but mainly by male authors. What these essays have afforded women, however, are chances to receive men's lectures on feminine virtues.

Almost all reprints and new publications, in effect, purport to shape the female mind in terms of how to be a woman for male interest and taste. Male essayists in the early twentieth century, while leading women's liberation and decrying foot binding and forced marriage, defined women largely from the male perspective. For instance, Zhu Ziqing conceptualizes woman solely through his erotic fantasy over her body (72–75). To Lian Shiqiu, a leader of the New Culture Movement, a woman is merely talented for threading the needle (38). To Yutang Lin, a woman "has no career except the career of wife and mother," and the ideal woman is the wise, gentle, and firm mother (154–55). Even Hu Shih, one of the pioneers in the post–May Fourth women's movement, in "Women Are Also Human" (*nüren yeshi ren*), originally a speech to the Woman Alliance Union, concludes that women's liberation improves *the family life* of the Chinese (42–43). A new essay collection, *Outstanding Women* (*jiechu de nüxing*), tells the stories of more than a hundred wives and mothers of famous statesmen, scientists, writers, and artists, praising the sacrifices these women have made for the successes of their husbands and children ("*Duocai*" 2). Essays on women often stress that a successful career woman should also create harmony in the family to keep her husband happy. Jia Pingwa, a renowned post-Mao male novelist, in "About Women," suggests that the world is still a man's world and that a woman can achieve her independence only through her understanding of men (72). Essays of a similar nature can be easily found in newspapers, magazines, or anthologies. For instance, the article "Why Does Mrs. Thatcher Prepare Steaks for Her Husband?" teaches that a woman's value lies primarily in her care of her husband (*Xinmin Evening News* 27).

For these political reasons, the essay for centuries remains largely a vehicle for male voices. The cultural and literary renaissance during the May Fourth period witnessed a boom in women's essays. Compared with their male counterparts, however, women's essays did not gain the same respect as writing models or the focus of study. Virtually, women's essays have been forgotten and erased from memory. Dooling and Torgeson notice "how much women's writing had been produced in the first decades of the twentieth century—and how little was readily available to readers in any language (even Chinese!)" ("Acknowledgement"). Under Mao, even though handling the double burden proved women's talents and abilities to use discourse conventions, the female essay did not come of age until the early 1990s when prolific post-Mao female writers secured their positions in the literary world with quality work. While a decade ago, women were limited to fiction and poetry writing, now they expanded their territory to the essay in which they started to speak to the public in their own voices, instead of through characters or events that could be read as only fictional.

This breakthrough in genre has largely enhanced the significance of women's writing, bringing about a revolution of women, within women, and for women. In this respect, essay writing can be regarded as the second wave of the post-Mao women's movement launched with fiction and poetry in the early 1980s. The essays translated into English for the first time in this anthology document post-Mao women's views in this pivotal era.

PRESENTING POST-MAO WOMEN'S ESSAYS

This collection presents post-Mao writers' perspectives on Chinese women's material reality as well as their purposes of writing fiction or poetry. Their essays are different, dissonant, and even divergent, as their perspectives represent the standpoints of urban women intellectuals in the new age of economic reform. The dominant theme of their essays is redefining and repositioning women, by reassessing the ideological framework of gender embodied in traditional feminine virtues as well as in social demands of women brought to the fore by commercialism and capitalism in economic reforms. From the rhetorical point of view, post-Mao women's essays maintain the traditional features of the genre: metaphorical and poetic, responding to sparks of illumination from readings or personal observations with optional organization and personal approach. Inquiring rather than concluding, most of these essays, whether long or short, keep questions open-ended and stress the thinking process rather than directly state the point. Each writer makes intellectual connections as her will dictates, making associations between the stories she has read and the life experience she has had, between the past and the present, as well as between others and herself. Stylistically, the structure grows out of the mood, tone, and purpose of the essay, sometimes formal and sometimes casual and accidental, while diction and turn of phrase demonstrate rhetorical adroitness.

To unravel the rhetorical complications of post-Mao women's feminist writing and to recognize that they are not a monolithic and hegemonic group despite their shared experience under and after Mao, each section showcases essays by one writer accompanied by her biography and an analysis of her feminist viewpoint. The order of the essays of each writer, however, does not reflect the order in which they were written, but instead is based on how these essays might received by a non-Chinese-speaking readership unfamiliar with their work.

While the chapters are arranged alphabetically by the writers' last names, the essays focus on three themes. The first theme revolves around the search for the definition of female writer (*nüzuojia*) and her writing—for example, Zhang Kangkang's "The 'Grand' Realm versus the 'True' Realm," Bi Shumin's "A Writer's Fate," and Shu Ting's "A Mirror of One's Own." The second theme centers on the writers' efforts in defining women independent of traditionally prescribed female virtues—for example, Lu Xing'er's "Women's 'Sameness' and 'Difference,'" Shu Ting's "The Shadow of the Chaste Temple," and Hu Xin's "A Pink Humor." Fang Fang's "On Women" echoes Lu Xing'er's and Hu Xin's criticism of the male definition of woman. The final theme evolves out of their concerns about the tension between women's self-realization and traditional gender roles. Clustered under this theme are Lu Xing'er's "Women and the Crisis," Shu Ting's "Give Her Some Space," Han Xiaohui's "Women Don't Cry," and others.

Expressing their views and concerns, these writers imagine, construe, and construct dimensions for women. They examine the types of writers they are, engage themselves in the rebellion against patriarchy, and seek possibilities for the kinds of women they, and others, can be. The essay provides the writing woman with spaces where she articulates herself more overtly than in fiction writing, resonating to a genre in which she projects her voice, her image, and her views. The female essay is by women, about women, and for women.

NOTES

1. Since the mid–1970s, China has been practicing the "one couple, one child" policy to control population explosion. Each urban family has one child except for twins. Ethnic minorities and rural families whose first children are daughters are allowed to have two children.

2. Zhang Kangkang, "We Need Two Worlds," in this book.

3. Jiang Yongping offers a comprehensive account of the problem (215–17).

4. See "Translator's Note" for Chinese woman naming.

5. The May Fourth movement was named after a student demonstration in Tiananmen Square in Beijing on May 4, 1919, against the Treaty of Versailles among the world powers to force China to hand the German-held concessions (the Shangdong peninsula) to Japan. The protest soon grew into a widespread patriotic movement, bringing forth a renaissance in culture and scientism as well as language and literature.

6. When doing research in China, I noticed that most Chinese publishers were interested in female writers' essays merely because of their prose styles and literary reputations. None of the publishers showed any interest in these writers' thoughts on gender. All women's essays on gender were scattered in anthologies on family, children's education, or femininity, easily escaping notice.

I

BI SHUMIN

Born in 1952, Bi Shumin grew up in Beijing. During the Cultural Revolution (1966–1976) when she was seventeen years old, she began to serve as a nurse and then as a physician in the military on the Kunlun Mountain in Tibet. Among the nine women soldiers on the snow-covered military base, she was the only one who served for eleven years, while the rest were either expelled for "inappropriate behaviors" (that is, intimate contact with or sexual harassment from male officers) or discharged after marriage. Bi became a professional writer after she received a master's degree in Chinese literature from Beijing Teachers' University. Later, she earned a doctoral degree in psychology.

Bi's life on the mountain ranges of the Himalayas and her observations of her male counterparts provided rich resources for her first fiction, "Kunlun Elegy" (*Kunlun Magazine* 4, 1987). This novel, along with others, has enabled her to win many literary prizes in both Taiwan and mainland China. Some of her fiction has been translated into English, such as "Broken Transformers," "The Hitchhiker," and "An Appointment with Death." Her novel *Saving the Breast* (2003) recounts how women cope with breast cancer. The essays translated in this anthology, except "A Writer's Fate," are chosen from Bi's essay collection *The Reminder of Happiness* published in 1996.

In China, Bi is critically acclaimed for articulating ideas through metaphor and expressing concerns about underprivileged women. Her own comments on the characters in her fiction, *Women Workers* (2004), echo one of her essays here, "When Can Women Start Enjoying Life?":

> I paid great attention to the factory women I worked with on a daily basis. I saw them aging beneath the uniform like withering flowers, while their beauty and youthfulness were gradually replaced by sparkling metal works and silver locks of hair on their foreheads. ("Bi Shumin")

15

Since the late 1980s, the women workers in Bi's fiction have been pushed aside by economic reform waves. While many fiction writers are chasing the tide by symbolizing the trendy, the modern, and the grandeur, Bi's works still center on women's daily lives, topics that even some Western critics consider out of date and no longer interesting, particularly to younger generations. However, a careful reading reveals that Bi's choice is not without purpose. Employing figures of speech in her essays and addressing the gender roles women are expected to play, Bi attempts to rekindle the hopes of women stricken by poverty and to strengthen the confidence of career women. She encourages women of younger generations to shake off the shackles of patriarchy that control their thinking about women's positions at home and in society and to become the amazing women she believes in.

A WRITER'S FATE[*]

As a child, I did not give much thought to what I wanted to be when I grew up. When asked to describe "my dream" in the composition class, I would choose some profession that appeared interesting to write about. Oftentimes my dream was becoming a farmer simply because it allowed me to add descriptive details about the seasons and colorful fields to meet the minimum word requirement.

My father devoted his life to the military. We had many books, but few of them were literary works. The majority were books on military affairs and the complete works of Marx, Engels, and Lenin. At a young age, I had already finished reading the military historiography series, *Prairie Fires Kindled by Sparks*. One day, when Father was discussing a battle [during the War against Japan] with his friends, and I cut in, speaking up like an adult, "If the Red Army could have prepared their food better [on the Long March], maybe fewer soldiers would have died." My family considered it disrespectful for a child to break in during grownups' conversations. But that day, Father did not get mad at me as usual. He only shot an odd look at me.

We also had a complete collection of the four literary classics.[1] They were displayed on the shelf like neatly laid bricks. I remembered how excited Father was when he bought these books, but I did not think he finished reading them. Many times, I heard him complain: "Is the relationship between Jia Baoyu and Lin Daiyu worth so much elaboration? Boring!"

I finished reading *Dream of the Red Chamber* when I was nine or ten years old. But there were many characters I did not know. For example, I would misread the character *xi* [袭] in the name of *Xiren* as "deaf" [聋],

[*] Originally published in the literary magazine *Jin Chao* [Golden Tides] 1 (1995): 50–51.

simply assuming that Baoyu's head-maid had hearing problems, without knowing that the name originated from the classical allusion, "as attractive as flowers."

In elementary school, I always received good grades on my essays. Many times, the teachers gave me A+'s. The trick I used was to make my writing different and lively. For example, once the teacher assigned us the topic "A Conversation to Remember." Many of my classmates wrote about conversations with their parents who educated or encouraged them. Some of them were more creative and wrote about the conversations with their parents that had solved conflicts or disagreements. But I had a different idea. I wrote about a phone conversation between a Chinese child and an African child. The teacher commended my writing. But I felt unworthy and embarrassed, even when I think about that essay today. How could the children communicate when they did not speak the other's language? Besides, the child in Africa was supposed to live in poverty. How in the world could he afford a telephone?

During the Cultural Revolution, the school library was virtually closed. I was attending a school in Beijing solely for students from families of elite social status. It was a beautiful campus with buildings of grand architectural style. The library was located in an old hall built in 1919. Sealed with steel bars, its tall windows looked like composites of small squares, through which the dim light cast an eerie glow. The librarian set up a rule: Students were not allowed to check out more books unless they submitted papers to criticize the books last checked out. No papers, no books. Now when I think about it, I reckon she was required to censor all the books in the library to get rid of "evil" ones. She could not do so much by herself and had to take advantage of the students. When the regulation was first implemented, many students participated. But usually after a book or two, they would quit, with only a few students continuing to check out books. It was not because we did not want to read, but because the rule was too burdensome. We were all thirteen- or fourteen-year-olds, restless and active when the Cultural Revolution was in its heyday. Who wanted to sit down and write papers? Each of us had a good time in reading, but none of us wanted the pain of writing hostile criticism. Honestly, people were too lazy to go through such troubles. I was lazy as well. Each time when I forced myself to write, I swore to myself that I would never check out any more books. But when I set foot in the library, I was exhilarated by the moldy smell, like an opium addict at the smell of the drug. I was busy walking and browsing among high shelves. When I approached the librarian, I had to lower my chin to hold the full load of books in my arms.

"Can you finish so many books?" she asked coldly.

"Yes, I can," I mumbled sheepishly.

"Can you finish so much writing?" she followed up.

"I can, too," I answered, without hesitation.

So the reading process became two phases. The first was full of pleasure—reading great Western novels—and the second was painful—writing. Ours was a boarding school with eight girls in a dorm room. At first, all of my roommates were enthusiastic about reading, but after a while, I was the only one who continued checking out books. When I brought books back to the room, my roommates fought to get ahold of them. But they left the writing to me. As if this was not bad enough, I had to wait to get books back from slower readers who could not finish in time. Once, a girl was still reading on the due date. I knew how bad it was to have your book taken away while you were in the middle of it. I did not have the heart to do so, even though her reading pace irked me. She was gracious enough to return the book before I asked, but she had a request: "I don't have time to finish it. Could you please tell me the rest of the story?" Her request turned me into a "storyteller" whose account also attracted other roommates. Afterward, they never asked me for books but wanted me to tell stories. At night amidst the riots in 1967 and 1968, in a quiet dorm room surrounded by a group of girls, I was telling beautiful stories to them, and to myself. . . . One of my roommates who is now living in the United States recalled that I told stories of Hugo's *The Man Who Laughs*, Tolstoy's *Anna Karenina*, Dickens's *A Tale of Two Cities* . . . (Honestly speaking, I am now stunned by my imprudence at that time. If it were today, I would not dare recount these classics, because their meanings are there for us to feel, not to express explicitly in words.) My friend told me she never read *The Man Who Laughs* herself. Believing the story I told was the best, she did not want to replace her beautiful memory with any other versions of the book, not even with Hugo's work itself. It was not because she did not like literature, but because she wanted to keep her childhood memories.

After reading and telling the stories, I had to go through the pain of writing. By "pain," I did not simply mean that I had to write so many Chinese characters when others were going out and having fun. The problem was that I loved these books but was required to trash them against my will. What could I write against? On the other hand, if I did not write, I could not read more books. I racked my brains frantically, and eventually, there I was, pleading with the ghosts of the greatest literary masters in the world for forgiveness: Dear masters, my bad mouthing of your works does not stand for my true feelings. I only want more chances to read your books. Please don't be mad at me.

However, even if not haunted by guilt, I still could not write, for I was unable to think of anything in the books that could possibly provoke any hostile criticism. In desperation, a trick popped up—I first used the clichés popular in the Cultural Revolution as my most striking claims and then quoted the books to show how they "dared" to send messages of "capitalist humanism." I cited long passages, writing each character with care and attention. When I turned in my writing, I was scared and nervous. To my surprise, the librarian commended my diligence. Only then did I find out that the number of words in the papers counted much more to her than the contents.

In retrospect, I feel grateful to the librarian who made me transcribe passages from great books to my papers and continuously provided me with invaluable "intellectual nutrition." This kind of education was almost impossible in those years.

I joined the military afterward, placing myself completely at the army's disposal. I did not get to be a telephone communication soldier as I had wished. The girl whose bed was adjacent to mine was assigned to the communication squad. I ended up working in a military hospital. While most of the enlisted girls were assigned to hospitals in urban areas, my fate sent me to Tibet. I did not complain, because to me Tibet was a mysterious place everybody wanted to visit, even twenty-some years back then.

Among the Himalayas, the most spectacular mountain ranges, the Gangdisé and the Gya La Gyirong, looked like buffalos carved in silver. Bowing their strong horns to the plains, they arched their muscular backs to lift up the skyline across the boundless tableland, stretching slopes up and down as far as the eye could see. It was there that I was stationed—the snow-covered mountain ranges of five-thousand-meter [over sixteen thousand feet in] altitude. There were nine girls among us, who were the first, and also the last, group of military women stationed on the high plateau of Tibet.

In an extremely arduous environment, the gender divide was erased. At forty degrees below zero Celsius [about seventy degrees below zero Fahrenheit], we trekked in nonstop blizzards, carrying more than fifty pounds of supplies on our backs, the same amount as the men's. Each day, we had to trudge for fifty kilometers [about thirty miles]. Each time when commanded to climb an icy mountain, I wished I had been dead. The hardship was inhumanely unbearable. Thinking I could not bear any more, I wanted to kill myself and had brooded over a plan for some time—I would fall off a cliff into some abyss and make the whole thing look like an accident. Nobody would know it was intentional because accidental deaths happened frequently during such arduous military training. My "accidental" death could make me a revolutionary martyr and would not cause any political trouble to my parents. . . .

My plan was perfect, but its realization was put off again and again. My feet did not obey my commands. I told my left foot, "step off the rock and be done with it." But my foot did not make it. Instead, it latched onto the crack between the rocks as if in fear of being pushed away by my hands. In honesty, my hands were numb and stiff, frozen as ice—I could not even move my fingers. How on earth could they do anything? I became mad at my left foot and turned to command my right foot, which did not obey me either.

Living was such an ordeal that I desperately wanted to die. I believed that the obstacles I was enduring were far worse than those the Red Army had experienced, but my body repeatedly refused to follow my orders. It was many years later that I realized that the resistance from my feet must have been my instinctive reaction of survival that saved my young life.

On that boundless high plateau, many young people did die. They had come from different regions but left their bodies and souls buried in Tibet forever.

My military life on the Tibetan Plateau lasted eleven years—the most precious years of my life.

When I retired from the military, I resettled in Beijing where I began to work as a physician in a factory. That year I was twenty-eight years old.

As a physician, I treated patients carefully. As a wife and mother, I took care of house chores and my child. For a woman, I believed, all these were important responsibilities.

Having almost accomplished what was required of me as a woman, I finally had some time to take in Beijing, the noisy and crowded capital city. Then I heard a sudden cry from my heart.

I had yet to realize a dream before leaving this world behind.

In my father's odd but meaningful look long ago, I saw his expectation of me: Someday I would speak my mind to the whole world.

Misreading the character *xi* as "deaf" and setting foot in the dark library had planted the seeds in my mind, preparing me for the dream step by step. Now if they had not had a chance to burst into life, they would have festered.

Fate sent me to the remote plateau where I experienced the most terrifying yet thrilling moments of my life. If I had not told these stories, I would have felt guilty for the rest of my life for erasing the memories of the young heroes whose graves were still under the deep icy snow.

So there I was, starting to write on a regular night shift at the clinic. My office with white walls and ether smell felt like a freezing cave. When patients came, I treated them, and after they left, I returned to writing. The ends of the old fluorescent tubes had burned black. Amidst its buzzing, I could feel the silence of the lonesome night.

My first novel *Kunlun Elegy* gained instant popularity, a successful debut for my writing career. But I did not think I had enough formal training, so I enrolled in a master's program in literature to study how great authors wrote. Now a professional writer in the headquarters of the China Metal-lurgical Industry Cooperation, where economic information floods in along with business events, I will probably write fiction about financial activities among the elite government officials. Of course, I will continue to write about soldiers on the Tibetan plateau, and being a wife and a mother, I will also write about women.

Writing is my fate, a fate that I can never escape.

NOTE

1. Referring to the vernacular novels *Dream of the Red Chamber, Journey to the West, The Water Margin,* and *Romance of the Three Kingdoms.*

ANDROGYNY

Walking in the street in front of me was a tall person in a ponytail and a bright floral shirt. Judging from the lovely slender figure, I was thinking: What a nice tall girl for modeling. That person suddenly turned around, and I saw a full bushy beard.

Coming in was another young person in a white polo shirt, blue shorts, and white tennis shoes with a haircut as short as a hedgehog's spines. If not for the bosom bouncing up and down like the ocean tides, I would not have known for sure it was a woman.

A female manager was sitting on a leather chair behind the desk, on which several telephones were blaring nonstop like fire trucks. Holding a handset, she was speaking firmly and briefly in simple syllables—"yes," "no," "okay"—in a strong voice that nailed her words down into the listener's mind with precision and power like the glittering metal heads of the thumb tacks on the wall map. Occasionally, some male employees would come in for business meetings. If not nervous and intimidated, they were, at least, kowtowing and listening.

I once saw a man crying in an expensive restaurant on a busy street where the fruit tea tasted like blood, thick and sticky. The man was talking about his ambition to be a senator, but the subject was not sad, and that restaurant was not the right place to cry in. In this respect, I believe women have better judgment. They cry only in the right place at the right time. Astonishingly, the man was shedding his tears like a storm, shooting them down onto his royal-blue tie in muffled sounds. At fifty, one should be able to make prophecies. This man must have accumulated worldly wisdom.

I have learned early on that if you cannot find a blouse in your size and color, try the men's section, where you can find incredibly rich colors and styles.

One of my male friends used to complain that he had to buy boys' shoes because his feet were small. Now he is happy. He told me his secret, "Things are better. I can buy women's shoes now." Shocked, I asked, "You don't mean you are going to wear high heels, do you?" "You mustn't have shopped in women's shoe stores for some time," he said, "Those flats with laces look exactly like men's shoes."

Both men and women wear jackets and silk scarves. There is no difference between the styles of men's and women's athletic shoes. Even senior male citizens walk in the streets in women's colors—purple, evergreen, and bright yellow. Men climb mountains, so do women. Men reach high goals, so do women. With the exception of sports, the gender boundary becomes more and more obscure, almost erased.

All my observations make me think about "neutrality [androgyny]."[1]

Neutrality can be viewed as the nature of some element. Alkali connotes deep bitterness and astringency, and acid sharp pains, but the neutrality between them leads to mildness and harmony. After centuries of confusion in which they searched for separate gender roles, men and women have finally begun to move toward something neutral—androgyny.

Androgyny is vision. Men and women are like a pair of eyes. Separated by the bridge of the nose, their vision of the world has enabled them and disabled them at the same time. In a society like a 3D dome theater, separated men and women cannot watch films through the stereoscopic glasses with one broken lens. Feeling nauseated and dizzy, they would have headaches. Androgyny serves as a pair of new glasses enabling both sexes to view things in harmony without distortion.

Androgyny is language. Living separately in their isolated tribes, males and females fight constantly, impossible to establish relations. Of course, they may have disputes over the border and hold cultural differences, but the different languages they speak cause the fundamental problem. Males speak an unpolished crude language, and females a tender, fine one. There are too many incomprehensible words to translate. Androgyny gives the united nations of sex a common language to prevent miscommunication.

Androgyny is a position in between. The tropical region is too hot, and the South Pole too cold. Only the place in between is mild and comfortable. Walking too far on the left or on the right of the road, we would be too close to the edge of cliffs. Only walking in the middle makes us feel safe. The bright sun blinds us, and heavy rains blur our view. Only in the dusk, when the wind calms down and the moon lightens up the sky, can we see far down the road and the scenic sights on both sides. Androgyny is a great living condition.

Androgyny is wisdom. Men and women argue endlessly about identity and social issues. Disbelieving that they are created from a rib, women want to prove that they are the backbone. This is why we had "iron girl troops" who thought they were the same as men. Men who have lost one of their ribs are disabled to some degree (I believe the rib was taken from the left chest just in front of the heart). In the open without protection, the man's heart is vulnerable. Wanting security and safety, men pretend to be strong and powerful to fool their enemies in hopes that the latter will not launch attacks. An androgynous person is a perfect human being who does not go to extremes or become arrogant. This person never acts without discretion or in shortsightedness. His/her nerves are tempered with steel. Utilized as strings, they can play beautiful music; utilized as chains on gears, they can lift the thick darkness on the earth to reveal the horizon.

Androgyny is courage. Since ancient times, men and women have emphasized differences in garments. Nowadays we are stripped of our exterior markers like commodities of their labels. We must rely on our interior beauty to speak up for ourselves. No longer does gender identity depend on colors or hairstyles. It gleams from every direction like a bright lantern in the dark. Androgyny provides a broad dark background against which our genders are displayed as beautifully as lustrous pearls.

Androgyny is elimination and simplicity, through which the human race returns to the primitive and the true. Both men and women will march toward the same destination. United, they will become the same human being with a pure soul, a significant human being in capital letters.

Androgyny is different from saying that women can do whatever men can do. This statement identifies women as a little boat managing to get close to the men's large ship. In contrast, androgyny is the lighthouse. Toward its welcoming lights both men and women move forward, helping and enabling one another, leaving no one behind.

Androgyny does not emphasize physical difference. For a long time, hard and strong muscles have decided what we do. Physiological differences have built insurmountable gender gaps. But human history is not a record of sports that separate males and females into isolated matching units. Madam Curie is recorded in history not by being Mrs. Curie, but by her discovery of radium. Li Qingzhao has a place in history not because of her beauty but because of the aspiration in her poetry—"Dismal . . . downcast . . . disconsolate"—and her ambition to "return after death as a ghost." History is like a furnace that refines the ore to reveal its invaluable contents measured by the amount, regardless of the form. Technology has bridged the gaps in physical build. The machine strengthens women's hands. Pressing electronic buttons, they can tear down massive objects. The computer does not care if hairy coarse fingers or long delicate ones punch its keys. Even wars are fought differently. The victories are not determined through physical fights with swords and spears but through intelligence technology thousands of miles away from the battlefield.

In an arena where willpower contests are held, the rule of "ladies first" does not exist any more. The Creator is not a compassionate gentleman but a warrior who respects only winners, no matter whether they are in skirts or suits.

When weighed on the scale of androgyny, women will receive neither prejudice nor special treatment.

Androgyny illuminates the world with the light of hope but also makes it challenging. No matter whether you like it or not, androgyny will unify the world and show the power of each individual.

NOTE

1. Bi uses *zhongxing* as a pun for both neutrality and androgyny.

WHEN CAN WOMEN
START ENJOYING LIFE?

When can women start enjoying life?

Before we answer this question for our mothers, our sisters, and ourselves, we must explain what women deem as enjoyment.

The enjoyment we refer to is not affluence allowing us to spend money at will, nor indulgence in extravagance, nor a pretentious lifestyle full of vanity, nor a powerful status allowing us to boss others around.

The enjoyment we refer to is not elegance lent by jewelry, nor delicate beauty rendered by silk and satin, nor boastful worldliness developed through luxury tours, nor even sensual indulgence in instrumental music.

The enjoyment we refer to is time we can give to ourselves—time when we can cook favorite food only for ourselves, shop around and buy lovely gifts for ourselves, go out with friends in the park without looking at the watch now and then for fear that it may be too late to prepare the family dinner or to get in the laundry we have hung out to dry[1] ... or watch a movie in the theatre without worrying about others' demands or needs.

Women's enjoyments we refer to are merely basic, normal human needs. However, countless women have forgotten their own needs because of their exhausting lives.

But how much women would like to enjoy life!

Nursing the baby, heating up milk, doing the laundry, a woman wipes away sweat beads from her forehead and says, "The baby is too young for me to think about myself. I'll be able to enjoy life when the baby grows up . . ."

The baby is growing older and now goes to the daycare. The woman, holding the toddler, does grocery shopping and prepares family meals. Meanwhile, she is also expected to be an outstanding employee at work. Busy and exhausted, she cannot even tell day from night and the sun from the moon.

Never mind, when the child attends elementary school, I'll have a break and enjoy myself . . . the woman says to herself, not realizing that the wrinkles have begun sprawling over her face.

The child finally reaches school age, but the woman is engulfed in more responsibilities.

Bring up my child to be an extraordinary person, the woman thinks to herself, spinning herself like a top around the workplace, the home, the grocery store, the school, and various extracurricular activities. . . . She rotates like a planet orbiting the sun—the husband and the child.

Gray strands of hair like silver threads now drape over the woman's fatigued forehead.

When can I have a break and enjoy life?

Asking herself this question on a moonless night, the tired woman stretches her sore back and limbs.

All right, just hang in there a little longer. When the child grows up and goes to college, or has a job, everything will be all right. By then, I can fully enjoy life. . . .

So the woman promises herself.

She then smiles in her dreams.

Time takes away beauty and energy from the woman, filling the void with wrinkles and slowness.

The child has grown up and flown out of the house like a bird out of its nest, leaving behind feathers of memory to accompany the mother.

The woman lets out a heavy sigh of relief. Finally, she has time to enjoy life.

Sadly, her loose, tender teeth do not allow her to chew hard food; her failing eyesight stops her from selecting pretty colors for herself. With hearing difficulties, she can no longer tell what sounds are distinctly beautiful; with weak legs, she can no longer hike high hills. . . .

Then her child returns home, bringing back a younger child.

The woman is now in a delirium, feeling she has traveled backward in time. Once again she resumes endless care and chores.

The younger child begins to learn to speak, but this time, the child calls the woman *nainai,* not "mama."

As such, the woman gets older and older, and eventually, she no longer thinks about enjoying life.

At the last moment, she remembers a promise she made to herself a long, long time ago: On a spring day, she would wear a red chiffon scarf and take a trip to the country. On the soft green grass, she would lie down in the sun and listen to ants crawling on rocks. . . .

What a marvelous enjoyment this is.

Says the woman, and puts herself to sleep, quietly and forever.

Please forgive me for drawing such a bleak and depressing picture of women's lives.

This is because I think that when a woman pours her love and care generously out to the world, she has neglected a significant person—herself.

Women, let us save some time and space for ourselves.

Don't put off what we want again and again. Don't wait forever.

Start to enjoy life now. Start today.

Don't forget yourself when you spoon-feed your child with the good food on the dining table. Don't forget yourself when you spend money on house decors and on the husband. Don't forget yourself when you devote your energy to your job. Don't leave out your name from the list of people to whom you want to give gifts. . . .

Good women, please start to enjoy life right at this moment.

NOTE

1. Most Chinese households do not have dryers due to a lack of supply and particularly due to high energy costs.

SEEKING AMAZING WOMEN

I am looking for amazing women.

Women constitute half of the world population. If there are six billion people, at least three billion of them are females, including senior ladies and female infants. If we think of females below thirty years old as girls, then about a fifth of the female population—sixty million people—are women.

Looking up at the clouds and sunrays and down at the massive crowds, I often wonder how many women can count as amazing.

The first and foremost quality of amazing women is compassion.

It is the most important component of integrity to counteract brutality in the world, which, filled with gun smoke and blood, is a battlefield of power, money, love affairs. . . . Under the mask of its amiable gentleness are murderous, bloodthirsty eyes. Amazing women can accomplish the mission of cleansing souls, purifying the world as aluminum sulfate purifies water. Despite obstacles, they function as lubricating oil to keep the wheels of history rolling. Their compassion provides resources for human affection.

How many compassionate women are there?

The number is not large in my estimate, though. It is hard for females to maintain compassion, because they have endured too much victimization and suffering. After being wounded, a woman tends to be obsessed with revenge that inflames her heart with hatred, which she utters at night with clenched teeth, placing curses on life and the world like a witch.

Forgive me, ladies. I would like to imagine that the majority of us are compassionate as if I could test a piece of metal and say it is 100 percent gold. But the truth is few women can remain compassionate after having suffered repeatedly as victims. The chances of finding these women are as slim as finding a crystal-clean creek that has rolled through foul, muddy waters. Some ferocious, niggling, wretched elderly ladies are my living proofs.

Second, amazing women are smart.

They are smarter than men because women are more gentle and tender. Intelligence is gold armor that provides women with self-protection before they set out to protect others. Women without intelligence are like translucent jellyfish without strategies to protect themselves or to make self-adjustments. They are like unguarded cities. Women's delicate hands can turn intelligence into a sword, with which they blaze paths overgrown with bushes and cut off the excessiveness. On the mysterious ocean, intelligence fuels women's ships like the wind filling the sails. With their intelligence, amazing women represent half the brain of the human race, expressing themselves in sonorous alto voices echoed across the land.

However, it is hard for women to obtain intelligence. Most of the time, they are clever without vision. Heavy makeup blinds their eyes, and narrow social circles restrict their imaginations, their senses dulled at sweet words. Lost, they sometimes go astray at crossroads. Intelligence is not only the soul endowed on us by God, but also a disciple of Wisdom, Experience, and Courage. It must be crafted through artwork like a piece of jade. This work depends much on opportunities as well.

All gemstones are not lustrous; all seeds do not grow into tall stately trees.

For this reason, the number of intelligent women is much smaller than we think. About this, I can be as certain as an experienced old farmer who knows for sure that wheat harvests do not come from barren soil.

Amazing women are brave. On planet Earth, even if there are no other problems, conflicts between the sexes always exist. They are forever entangled in fights against each other yet are inseparable like strands braided into a rope. If you are an amazing woman, no matter where you sail your ship, you will, sooner or later, meet a good man. But do not take it for granted that you can dry your soaked body on parched haystacks. When you walk in the streets, do not expect to find shelter under the eaves of an old house that may protect you from the rain. Before you know him well, a man will offer generous help. When you are better than him, the man will treat you seriously. Who knows if this is a fortune or misfortune to amazing women? Compassionate, smart, and brave women, muster your courage to walk and sing alone at night. You must swim across an unexplored river like a mermaid, when there is no bridge, no boat, and even no birds.

How many such amazing women can we find?

Thinking about the shrinking number, I do not have the heart to make my sieve meshes too tight. Women seem born intimidated and are as shy as sensitive plants that close their petals upon touch. So do not make excessive demands of women.

Now only a few women are left to continue climbing the ladder.

Last but not least, amazing women are beautiful.

It is cruel to require women to remain beautiful after they have gone through many ordeals on their life journeys. It is like hoping flowers to remain intact after a thunderstorm has struck them.

But women do want to be beautiful. To them, beauty is the primary element of charisma. Women who are not beautiful betray the Creator. Instead of beautifying the world, they pollute it.

What is "beautiful"? Different people have different answers. I can only offer my two cents' worth here.

Beautiful women are in perfect harmony—harmony in the face and the figure, harmony in the body and the soul. But harmonious beauty is not simply a good combination of fine physical features, but a presentation of the whole. Even flaws constitute harmony, like the shadow of laurel bushes on the moon.[1] Isn't the bright moon a great artistic inspiration for imagination, by the way? Harmony also purifies the soul, making inside beauty shine outward.

Beauty also means mildness. Spiciness and noisiness are far from beauty; they are stimulants for excitement. The beauty of remarkable women is like the gentle breeze caressing the world with warmth. On the other hand, it is enthusiasm like a bonfire, whose flames wave their long arms like bright red fall maple leaves and soft satins. Embodied in the enthusiasm is affection and graciousness.

Beautiful women live forever. Transient beauty does not reside in humans but in material objects. Beautiful women in their teens are as pure as morning dews, and in their twenties as luxuriate as oak trees. When they reach middle age, they look elegantly serene. In their senior years, they are rivers joining the ocean, calmly slowing down yet reviving.

Beautiful women transcend time and age, which are not their enemies but their representatives. When time goes by, it allows women to form and transform their beauty in different ways, developing from ingeniousness to profoundness.

As such, women's beauty is not a single-candle-lit lantern but an ever-burning gaslight.

Time may brush away rosy hues from women's cheekbones, but it provides women with unfailing components—integrity—as a gift. Unfortunately, some women do not value it as much as they should.

I say all remarkable women are beautiful.

So far I have built a pyramid to classify women.

Now how many amazing women remain on the top? Only a handful.

Are my criteria too high? Am I too pessimistic? Am I so picky that I have exaggerated women's weaknesses? Or should we simply forget about separating the amazing from the ordinary?

The modern world demands the best and the finest from us. Nowadays, women who shop for purses want to buy brand names of top quality. Why don't they want to be the best then?

Amazing women are like the top of an iceberg. Only the top fraction of its massive mount appears above water. So only a few women can reach the top. In the rest, we only find the defected or the ordinary.

Why shouldn't women have compassion the way they have eyes? Aren't women without intelligence like birds with broken wings? To women, aren't the qualities of persistence, bravery, and tenacity as important as pretty clothes? Don't women value their beauty the way old ladies value their last tooth?

For a better world, for our own perfection, and for the everlasting universe, let us all strive to be amazing women.

NOTE

1. An allusion to Mao Zedong's poem, "Reply to Li Shuyi."

II

FANG FANG

Fang Fang was born in 1955 in Nanjing, the capital city of Jiangsu Province. After working as a stevedore loading and unloading cargo ships for four years during the Cultural Revolution, she passed the college entrance examination in 1978 and subsequently received her bachelor's degree in Chinese from Wuhan University in 1982, the same year she published her first novel, *On the Wagon* in *Yangzi Arts and Literature* (*Changjiang wenyi*). Her other novels include *Hint, The Sunken Ship, Random Expressions, Landscape,*[1] and many more. She serves now as the editor of Hubei Television Channel in Wuhan City, director of the Hubei Writers' Association, and director and editor-in-chief of the magazine *Today's Celebrities.*

The essays include here are selected from her collection *Go Sightseeing.* In her essays, Fang Fang's political sensitivity toward women's gender consciousness under the paternalistic system agrees with her attitude toward life. Her advice to female college students is "When people tell you that marrying rich is better than working your way up, don't believe them." When asked why most male characters in her fiction are disappointing, while female characters are tragic, her answer was "because in reality men disappoint me. Although I am not a feminist, I am definitely a 'superwomanist.' . . . Many books teach women how to please and flirt with men to win their approval, but I am unable to do so. I believe in women's wisdom, and I write about women living at the bottom of society" ("Speech").

Given her background and position, Fang Fang's work provides readers with the powerful imagery of metaphor. Yet it is *how* she employs imagery that speaks loudest. Critical of the Chinese literary tradition that constrained its female writers within the boundaries of sceneries—"winds, flowers, snows, and moonlight"—Fang Fang instead turns that tradition upon itself to urge her readers to look closely at both its female writers and their texts

35

in the spirit of emancipation. Readers will find that spirit of rebellion in the simple beauty of her pen—a pen poised as a "sharp scalpel" in contrast to the "silk handkerchief." Fang Fang's writing also invites her female readers to learn how they may unwittingly work to harm womankind by employing patriarchal criteria to judge each other. Her insights offer valuable lessons that reveal complicated systems of oppression, which have worked so well only in that they have been hidden from women in what has been the "true victory for men."

NOTE

1. This novelette is available in English in *Contemporary Chinese Women Writers*, vol. II (Beijing: Panda Books, 1991), 18–135.

OBEDIENCE VERSUS DISOBEDIENCE

For thousands of years, Chinese literature grew in vigor, but women's literary voices were choked, thin and weak, because they were forced into a low social position for such a long time. Born at a disadvantage, women were forbidden to travel away from home. As a result, they did not have sophisticated knowledge to compose powerful literary works. They were not allowed to make appearances in political and civic events, whose ups and downs were exclusively men's business. Without the similar experiences and the philosophic sorrow about power politics, women were unable to compose political and critical prose as poignantly and compellingly as men. More important, women did not have chance to access progressive ideas and social trends, so their works could warrant high-level rational thinking. Like caged birds, women lived a confined and restricted life. Gradually, their desires to fly freely diminished, and so did their flying ability. No matter how frequently the outside world was shaken by riots, wars, uprisings, changes of dynasty, and political events, few of women's literary works reflected them. Bound painfully by tradition, women were vexed by their lot. Even talented women's writing is limited to personal woes and yearnings. For centuries, women's writing merely articulated anguish and grief. Literature came to be a silk handkerchief to wipe away women's bitter tears from their cheeks. Their writing rarely presented the maturing process of adolescents, or transcendental nihilism, or the awakening of solitary thinkers. This literary situation lasted until the May Fourth era, when Chinese women developed an awareness of their social conditions.

The years since the May Fourth era have seen women actively, or sometimes involuntarily, involved in sociopolitical, economic, and cultural events, moving from the private domain to the public arena, a new world offering new perspectives. Women began to realize that the metaphor for their figures—"more gracile than a day lily"—reflected the lackluster and sluggish life they were forced to live. Looking back at the painful past, women mobilized themselves in high spirits to fight for gender equality. Their spirit of disobedience became their courage, with which women wrote *whatever they wanted to*.

Of course, some writing of today's women still focuses on sceneries—winds, flowers, snows, and moonlight—topics to which men want to limit women's writing as well. But a majority of women are no longer satisfied with the limitations; they know they have the same rational thinking ability as men and are able to write whatever men are able to. Their exposure of wicked humans is more striking than male writers', and their description of nature reveals more meanings than men's. When women write about office politics, they describe cold-blooded brutality in meticulous detail. Their pens, like scalpels, cut open men's innermost thoughts that men themselves dare not to talk about. While men approach sexuality in elusive understatements, women write about it candidly with sincerity and honesty. For women, literature is no longer a silk handkerchief but a sharp scalpel to dissect everything they touch upon. The transformation in women's writing has shocked and terrified many people, particularly men who are used to traditionally defined females. Many of these men shake their heads at, show pity to, sneer at, take a "high road" around, or simply marginalize the women who dare to write whatever they want to.

In my point of view, today's women writers demonstrate an invaluable spirit of rebellion, which grows out of the deep oppression they have endured. The longer the oppression, the more forceful rebellions are. This is a natural process of women's emancipation, a process in which women develop their literary ideas into mature products. As a matter of fact, their literary rebellion that has elicited public worries or uneasiness is nothing more than a message that women writers want to send: They are no longer obedient females but *such women* as they present in their writings. Nothing but such women is all they want to be.

WOMEN'S EYES

I believe that women and men view the world differently. Compared to men, who enjoy the rulership on top of the hierarchy, boast of glorious deeds, or make comments on world affairs, women are more willing to hold out their warm and gentle hands to touch up and clean up the world. I have all the reasons to believe that women adjust themselves to the real life more easily than men, because they can form a bond with the exterior world.

We are also aware that, compared to men, women seem born distinctly disadvantaged. The sex differences make women's life journey much tougher than men's. If they want to obtain self-fulfillment, women have to fight much harder than men, especially when they want to express their views on nature, society, and humanity. Sometimes, it is not even easy for women to work outside the home. For these reasons, history has come to function as a documentary film. Its canons are exclusively men's, while women are just making appearances. However, women do not simply observe the development of canons in depression and misery. They leave home in tenacious spirits and paint the world with the colors reflected from their eyes. The diverse colors vividly project women in motion with determination and courage.

Women's views on life are as profound as men's, but are expressed in a peaceful and gentle voice, not in a radical manner. In such a distinct voice, women express their concerns about life and their love for life, without letting pain and suffering distress them. Wherever their voices echo, restless minds find peace.

At this, I remembered what a poet has written: To a man's eye, life is living; to a woman's eye, life is her identity.

ON WOMEN

Nowadays, a certain view is popular. If a woman expresses herself directly and candidly, nails down her thoughts concisely, and acts decisively, people call her "man" or "superwoman,"[1] no matter how many house chores she does, how much love she devotes to her husband, or how patient and responsible she is toward her child. If a woman speaks in a strained thin voice, acts hesitantly, looks sheepish, reserves—instead of speaking out—her ideas, or even if she does speak, cannot get to the point without beating around the bush (most times such indirectness is considered an art), people applaud her for being "Miss Femininity" or the "perfect Oriental lady." Such a woman often talks about how much she enjoys cooking, knitting, and waiting on her husband. People talk about the former group negatively but about the latter favorably. Not only do men hold this popular view, but women themselves as well.

However, there is no standard to judge whether or not a woman behaves like a woman. The view that in order to enhance her femininity, a woman should be soft-spoken, act coyly and submissively, move deliberately, remain reserved, and display her charm for men, not for herself, is a traditional women-molding framework that men created according to their own desires thousands of years ago. For thousands of years, the male-centered, patriarchal system has been suppressing women's natural development. The suppression evolving generation after generation has distorted the woman's own understanding of herself. Eventually, the woman not only agrees with men but also consciously molds her natural self within the framework, which she now uses as the criterion to judge other women. She now believes that women so defined and molded represent the ideal female. My living proofs are those women who often offer advice on how a woman can become attractive to men and how to look like "Miss Femininity." Keeping male satisfaction in mind, they have employed all sorts of cosmetics to dress up the "little woman" [*xiao nüzi*]² to indulge male tastes, while entirely erasing the memories of violence, oppression, and restrictions women suffered from men many years ago. What a true victory for men, and what a misfortune for women!

In China, women are categorized into "classy chamber ladies" [*dajia guixiu*] or "precious home maidens" [*xiaojia biyü*] based on their social status and literacy development. Material reality and the media demonstrate that the first group of women often think, speak, and act on their own will. Well-educated and with a strong sense of individuality, each of them has acquainted herself with democracy and freedom at a young age. They have often lived a well-off life and acquired literacy through the help of their educated parents. For example, many female leading figures of the New Cultural Movement in the May Fourth period³ were from this group. They fought against gender prejudice and restrictive conventions, firmly establishing themselves on the stage of life. Today, most women from the families of similar sociocultural status still maintain individual wills and a strong sense of equity. They want to retain autonomy (here, I am referring to their spirits and characters and not implying that they want to live an unmarried life) and develop their self-identities. These women do not want to subject themselves to men's control but rather to work with men on an equal basis. They quest for truth and humanity, not men. They may not appeal to men sexually, but they are true women who represent females through their outstanding work; they are role models for other women.

The second group, "precious home maidens," serve as men's pets, particularly less educated men, who greatly appreciate the femininity these women display. Nonetheless, this group does deserve some credit. Constrained by their living conditions and limited by their beliefs in their fate, these women have learned to exercise self-control at an early age and are able to use the appropriate rhetoric when dealing with various people and situations. Well-versed in customs and rituals, they have learned how to maneuver cunningly in different situations. They are suitable for family life—practical and useful. Examining them rationally, we can understand that these women are the results of oppression, of which they themselves may not be aware. Growing up without influence of the New Culture, their nature, like tree branches, has been framed and twisted since childhood, resulting in flawed personality development. Most of the time, they develop themselves according to the wishes of their parents, who are often beneficiaries or messengers of traditional values. Under the guidance of tradition, these women even believe that they are born women and should "behave" like women. When they finally have chances to contact progressive views, they have already formed their own rigid philosophy of life and worldviews. As a result, they cannot rid themselves of the mentality and demeanors of the "little woman." Even though men are attracted to them, the second type are not progressive women.

If a woman wants to liberate herself and win independence, she should follow the first group. If a woman only wants an easy life and men's cheers, she may join the second group. But I must tell the truth: Society advances, and China will eventually catch up with developed countries. By that time, their access to education and cultures will provide more room for women to develop themselves, and the membership of the "Little Women's Club" will decline. This prospect will disappoint men but encourage women.

NOTES

1. *Nü qiangren*, originally a positive term, has gained negative connotations. See more discussions of superwomen in Lu Xing'er's essay, "On Femininity."

2. Used as a contrast to "big gentleman," a term evolving from the idiom *nanzihan, dazhangfu,* meaning a "manly man, big-hearted guy."

3. See note 5 in "Introduction."

MAY MY DREAM COME TRUE

A magazine polled whether or not women wanted to be "full-time wives." Surprisingly, many women responded affirmatively—they were willing. Many of the respondents were even college graduates. The answer poses a dilemma for us who fight for women's liberation. On the one hand, it is indeed hard for women to meet professional demands because they seem to be born with additional domestic responsibilities—taking care of their children, their parents, and house chores. On the other hand, without income of their own, women cannot achieve financial independence. And without financial independence, women's liberation stays merely as empty words.

Many years ago, Chicago women forcefully appealed for liberation, articulating every woman's hope in the world. Yet women's liberation remains an unsolved issue, though frequently discussed. Women themselves certainly want to walk out of the home as masters of their own domains, even if they have to stretch the limitations of their female physiology to handle the exhausting demands of the job and the home. Men, however, always want women to return home.[1] They use the Japanese as a model, saying that Japanese men reach their arms to the front (the outside) to hold the world, while their women bend their arms to the back (the inside) to hold the world. The outside and inside complementary roles create a balance where the family functions the best. But in China, most men have to stretch their arms outside as well as inside, and so do their women; both sexes are worn out under the double burden. As a consequence, no one takes good care of the child. The foundation of the Chinese family is now shaky, and in some serious cases, the family is in shambles.

The reason behind men's position is that once women draw back their tired hands to the inside, men can reach both their hands outside. While women recognize some credit in men's proposal, they hold opposing views. They cannot return home because they are aware that in a culture dominated by traditional values, a woman's loss of economic independence means the loss of independence and free will. When she has no choice but to rely on her husband completely for a living, patriarchy would put her under huge mountains of oppression. This condition is more painful and much worse than physical weariness. Women who have been liberated from centuries-long suppression never want to go back.

The reality has caught both sexes in a dilemma.

Is there a solution? Even in a dream?

In their dialogue, [Daisaku] Ikeda and [Arnold] Toynbee propose: Mothers, like other educators, ought to be paid a salary; the salary ought to be high, and it ought to be paid directly to the mothers themselves. This way, mothers would be placed in a social status equal to that of professors or judges.

This is an encouraging prospect. Just imagine this: Mothers would be treated as professionals with their own income. They could stay at home with peace of mind and devote themselves wholeheartedly to their families without financially depending on their husbands. They would regard raising children as a mission and a cause, love this profession, and try their best to do it well. They then could take care of all domestic affairs—housework and the children's education including extracurricular activities—anything that could possibly happen to the family. This arrangement could also solve men's dilemma. Maybe we would not even need daycares or kindergartens. . . .

Extend the imagination further: When a woman gave first birth at twenty-five, she would have the next fifteen years to develop her mothering career with a higher salary than other professionals. During these years, she would get pay raises or cuts depending on the quality of education she provided to her children as both a mother and a schoolwork tutor. She would have a lot of time to prepare special lesson plans for the young, whom she could guide according to their talents and interests. She could spend a lot of time taking them to parks or on trips to see the outside world. Educated so well, the young minds would be open, and their knowledge and intellect would be enhanced. At the same time, the mother could prepare herself for a profession outside the home when she turned forty. If she were to retire at fifty, she would still have ten years to make contributions to society by working outside the home. The fifteen years of mothering could also provide her with the opportunity to learn a trade she is interested in. I assume that should this prospect become reality, there would be more excellent children in our society and more women mature in their professional development. In addition, the quality of the society as a whole would increase substantially.

I understand, however, that it is impossible to implement this proposal unless we are a well-developed society. Even in an extremely wealthy country, it may exist merely as a dream. But how much I hope this dream comes true!

NOTE

1. Chinese women were required to work outside home for socialist construction under Mao (1949–1976). See the "Introduction" for the backdrop of this remark.

III

HAN XIAOHUI

Han Xiaohui is an essayist and the editor-in-chief of literature for *Guangming Daily* in Beijing. When she graduated from middle school in 1970 during the Cultural Revolution, she was assigned to a factory where she worked for eight years before she enrolled in the Department of Chinese Literature at Nankai University in Tianjing, Hebei Province, in northern China.

Han's first essay was published in 1974, followed by novelettes and more essays. Among all her collections, Han thinks *Something to Say to You* and *The Happy Buddhist* best represent her views on literature, humanity, political culture, and gender. Her other essay anthologies include *Bribery, Bribery, Out of Swamps, Self-Ridicule, Heart to Heart, Embarrassment Experienced, Women Don't Cry*, and *Essays of Han Xiaohui*.

Specifically for this English anthology, Han wrote to share her perspectives on women and women's literature. She believes that gender equality must be built on the belief that both men and women are humans. Sadly, she points out, gender equity still remains a myth in reality, in spite of the "flying flags of equity" everywhere, particularly in recent years. As an educated woman, Han feels that gender inequality is rooted deeply in every aspect of life—political and economic culture, social values, human rights and the humanity, mindset, and ideology—in Chinese society. She points out that in this modern age, the journey to women's true liberation has only just begun. It is a tough journey of the unknown, a journey of ups and downs as well as ambushes and obstacles.

Therefore, Han thinks that literary women must bear the responsibility for women's liberation by thinking about gender equality and emphasizing it in their writing. Women's literature must tell the truth about women's material lives. Han regards it as an improvement in creative writing that women writers have legitimized the subject matters of life, the soul, emotions, and lifestyle, including even those of "little women" and private life, topics that have been hitherto excluded from Chinese essay writing, a traditionally male genre to express men's passions toward national politics and military affairs. Women's expansion of prose topics has brought themselves back to life in flesh and blood. Now women can express sorrow and happiness as well as hopes after so many years of deception when they were ballooned beyond reality into an empty revolutionary image in Mao's era. Han warns, however, that women's literature is far different from the writing about "little women," a kind of writing that offers advice on how to observe female virtues with regard to relationships and family life without meaningful insight into women's concerns in terms of their broad social needs. Although Han is not against the writing of "little women," she refuses to produce this kind of writing. In her perspective, the term "women's literature" must be carefully examined, as it is now mistakenly used to promote writings about "little women" or all women's writings. Han writes: "Strictly speaking, in literary creation, there should not be a divide between male and female writing. Literary criteria are the same for both sexes. The difference lies in quality, not in the sex. This is my principle." The principle for women's literature applies to all literary works, regardless of the writer's sex. Han's literary goal, then, is "write to move the world as well as the soul."

GENDER ROLES IN COMMERCIALS*

At a gathering of friends, one of our topics touched upon today's commercials.

"Commercials are now everywhere," one said and then cleverly raised two questions to tease our minds:

"In commercials, what do most women do? What do most men do?"

Her questions were like a wake-up call: Needless to say, women, particularly middle-aged women, are mostly designated the roles of cooking, laundering, cleaning the bathroom, mopping, and tidying up rooms. . . . A liquid detergent is even named "Mama." The most insulting was a TV commercial for a washer, wherein ladies were so happy after using it that they started dancing, as if they had been the Wilis in *Giselle* who received special blessings from God. As for men, the camera lens catches them rolling in triumph behind the wheels of luxury cars or upon returning home, parading to the dining table full of fancy food and wine under the admiring gaze of the wife and children.

No wonder my daughter often exclaims, "It's much better to be a man who doesn't have to do any chores!"

This message is not only transmitted to children, but also to **adults**, be they male or female. This is our society's belief, a belief that even dominates writers' seminars.

A woman asks a man, "You don't look as well as before. Why doesn't your wife take good care of you?"

The man answers, "Recently, she's been too busy with her work to take care of me."

---

* Written in 1997, this essay appeared in Han's collection *Women Don't Cry*.

A man asks a woman, "Who is cooking for your husband and child while you are here at the conference?"

The woman answers, "Before I left, I cooked a lot. The fridge was stocked full of raw and cooked food."

With these greetings and exchanges, no one feels anything wrong. But if the roles in the questions had been reversed, would we have felt odd?

The answer is obvious. Even children would say, "Of course!" I have proof in one of my daughter's drawings that has been imprinted in my memory forever. She drew the picture when she was four years old. When she came running, I was doing the laundry, my hands deep in detergent bubbles in the sink. My heart churned when I looked at the picture: I was on the left, buried in a pile of dirty laundry. In the middle was Daughter, who was playing with her teddy bears and dolls, and on the right was the man, with his feet up, watching TV on the couch. Children's thoughts are keenly clear—they are conscious of what happens in society that determines what to think. Children are influenced by the values the adult world imparts to them, not to mention the bombarding effect of TV commercials.

In spite of the thinking I have done, I have made many mistakes in guiding my daughter. I do not know how they have happened, but they are the most stupid, utterly wrong words I have ever spoken. Most of the time, I just mouth them naturally:

"You are a girl. If you don't learn how to do homemaking, how can you have a future?"

"You are a girl. Speak softly. Don't make people jeer at you!"

"You are a girl. Move gently like a lady."

"You are a girl. . . ."

Ay-ya-yay! These warnings bursting out one after another are hurting my eardrums. All clichés—nothing new. The moderns have not added anything new since our ancestors prescribed these comprehensive restrictions. For example,

> A girl at the age of ten ceased to go out (from the women's apartments). Her governess taught her the arts of pleasing speech and manners, to be docile and obedient, to handle the hempen fibers, to deal with the cocoons, to weave silks and form fillets, to learn (all) woman's work, to furnish garments, to watch the sacrifices, to supply the liquors and sauces, to fill the various stands and dishes with pickles and brine, and to assist in setting forth the appurtenances for the ceremonies (*Li Ji* [Book of Rites], *Nei Ze* [the Nei She]).[1]

When walking, don't look back. When speaking, don't show the teeth.

When sitting, don't move the knees. When standing, don't sway the skirt. When happy, don't laugh out loud. When angry, don't raise the voice. The inside and outside are separate places for females and males. Don't peer at the outside; don't walk out of the chamber. Cover the face to steal a glimpse at things; hide the figure before going out (*Nu lunyu* [Analects for Women], *Lishen zhang* [On Posture]).[2]

My goodness. Am I glad that these old restrictions are obsolete today! Otherwise, how would it be possible for me to write essays?

However, thanks to these old conventions that used to restrict us, we have learned not to impose "new commandments" on our daughters.

Thanks to the lessons we have learned from the old tradition, we know that no one has the right to appoint us to be "Mama" or roles similar to the one in the detergent commercial.

At the same time, I want to make a disclaimer: I, Han Xiaohui, am not a "feminist."[3] My humble opinion disagrees with some extremist views, such as those that even wonder if men can give birth. Although a modern career woman working outside the home, I never neglect the domestic responsibilities that tradition assigns me. I do almost everything—laundering, cooking, knitting, carrying rice sacks, and replacing the propane tanks for the stove. I even dug out underground storage to preserve vegetables for winter years ago. I have done the best I can, believing I should shoulder responsibilities. What I want to say is that society has moved toward the electronic age of science and technology, leaving behind the backward agricultural economy in which men used to plow and women to weave. The question is: Should we also change the traditional mindset about gender roles like "men handle the outside, and women handle the inside" along with the scientific and technological development? By stating this, I am not bargaining. Just think about how many people in our society are still illiterate or semi-literate. These people may follow the media as a moral and legal guide. Think again about gender inequality in our society, and we can see the persuasive power of these nonstop, bombarding commercials.

Lastly, let me end on a lighter note: Don't discriminate against men. When women are assigned to so many house chores, how can men show off their talent? Aren't we depriving them of the chance to compete for the title of Model Husband?

NOTES

1. Original documentation of the source. Translation adopted from *Li Chi: Book of Rites*, translated by James Legge (New Hyde Park, NY: University Books, 1967), 479.

2. My translation.

3. See "Introduction" for an analysis of this disclaimer.

I DON'T WANT TO BE A WOMAN [*]

My seven-year-old daughter is holding her hands behind, leaning tightly against the wall like a sculpture, saying no. Though silent, she lifts up her head, darting angry glances at me every now and then. Today, she should have practiced the piano, but she sneaked out to play hit'n-turn[1] with a group of boys her age from whom even dogs would have shied away. Hitting and turning cards nonstop on the muddy ground, she is covered in dirt but comes back home in high spirits, her outfit like a brush painting of mountains and rivers, her face fiery red, and her eyes beaming with excitement. I can fully imagine her unflinching ferocity when she is playing against the boys.

Insanely mad, I start nagging and suddenly hear myself saying, "How can a girl be so wild?"

Before I even finish what I am saying, I regret it. But Daughter, at my words, is already protesting,

"What about a girl?"

I ran out of words.

That "I don't want to be a woman" is what I always want to get off my chest.

Actually, this is just a subtle way to articulate my thoughts. What I really want to shout out is: "I hate you, God! It's unfair of you to put me in a female body!"

Oh, my God, what is with you? Aren't you afraid that men will condemn you for not being feminine, obedient, exquisite, attractive, and contented?

---

[*] Written in October 1991. Official publication information unavailable.

These days, men are said to prefer "real women" who are supposedly "loving and obedient." When men single out a woman for not behaving like a woman, she is doomed.

At the same time, though, I can clearly hear female kinfolks' endless sighs of complaint about their fate.

"Still mad at me?" I reach out to stroke Daughter's head, trying to soften the tension.

Quickly, she squirms away. Pursing her lips, she does not let me off the hook: "You said you hated it when people were saying a girl should behave this way or that way!"

Feeling chills run down my spine, I grin helplessly. Yes, I did say so.

I have hated this advice to girls ever since my childhood. Each time I raised my voice in excitement when playing games, I could hear a reprimand in whisper:

"A girl should not act so wild!"

This was my grandma's voice. She was a lady who observed all traditional female virtues, living a life of austerity and chastity without provoking any rumors or criticism. Behaving herself, she never talked loudly and was always caring and nurturing. However, her wings were so tightly folded that no air could get through. Whenever I stretched my neck to peer at the outside world, she covered me up with her wings and spoke gently:

"Hui, my baby, it is for your own good."

For my own good?

What about it was for my own good?

I don't know if it was God's intention or human's misunderstanding that Eve was created from one of Adam's ribs. Since then, generations of women have come to be men's subordinates.

Normally, we do not like telling old stories again and again. Yet this old story, despite its ceaseless repetition, has yet to finish its first chapter. In the sunshine of the twenty-first century, women will not only lose their enthusiasm for progress but also suffer from a new decease—the deficiency in the spirit of being women.

How long and how painful this illness is!

Talking about family contributions?

Now men have more and higher demands. They want women to be not only their wives but also their mothers, maids, and mistresses. . . .

Self-sacrifices?

These lead to a bottomless abyss, an endless process where women burn themselves out like candles or die as silkworms making cocoons; they do not see any changes in the world they live in. Yet the sun and the moon, mountains and rivers, and the Earth and the other planets continue their old ways without care.

Pains?

About them women cannot even find a confidant to talk to. Like talking to the winter wind, whatever they say cannot change anything—winds, rains—nothing.

All that is left is sorrow and sadness.

Sadness is no worse than the dying heart.

"Now, go have supper," I am waving Daughter away in weariness, not wanting to reason with her.

"No, I won't," Daughter is stuck in her stubbornness, her eyebrows close-knit and her chest heaving up and down, as if she was misjudged.

"So, what do you want?" I raise my voice, unconsciously.

She returns to her motionless sculpture-like posture.

My mother comes over and says, "You are more hard-headed than your mom when she was little."

I feel my heart jump at these words, and the chills attack me again. What is wrong with me? Didn't I hate people who wanted to control my mind as a little girl?

Thousands of times, I asked my grandma, "Why can't a girl have a slingshot, play marbles, or climb walls?"

At my question, Grandma would lower her eyes and utter a soft sigh, "Fate. The fate to be a girl, the fate to be a woman. . . ."

"So? If I don't accept my fate?"

Grandma would shoot me her famous angry look in return. Any girl who had received the look would automatically go through several days of self-chastisement. Grandma's suppression of my natural development has turned me into a good girl. I can feel her watching me from Heaven all the time and everywhere I go—interviews, meetings with writers, conferences, or gatherings with my friends. I cannot help but ask her if I am a good girl now.

I have imposed a mandate on myself not to break Daughter's heart.

But it is her little heart that I don't understand. Is it some unrealizable self-dignity that makes her mad at boys and yet envious of them at the same time?

Today, the Sun[2] looks different from yesterday. I cannot tell if it is because men have lost their sensitivity or because women are confused.

The sky is no longer as blue as before.

One can hear men bemoan their vulnerability, growling and shouting loudly, "Science and technology have turned women into men. . . ." Even well-known, kind men and prestigious scholarly journals now seriously discuss "husbands under their wives' tight control," "husbands in aprons," "feminism," "the psyches of dysfunctional families," etc.

In fact, nobody should be so nervous. The Moon does not intend to outshine the Sun.

It takes great courage to reveal this well-known secret. As a woman, I know I should appear frail, delicate, and incapable of holding the world. Every woman should be looking for a man, the Great Wall. It would be the uttermost happiness to rely on him with a sense of security. I am supposed to be scared to stroll alone late at night and should give myself willingly to him who could take me wherever he goes.

However, this is a dream that will never come true because he is also dreaming of coming with me wherever I go.

Bad wish. I must muster my courage to move forward by myself, while my heart quests in weeping sadness: When did men become such weak dwarfs, vain and irresponsible? They have lost manliness, without the courage to accept women who are willing to be their love laborers.

The worst is that countless men who cannot sustain their strength resort to oppressing women in order to hide their incapability as well as to console their loss of dignity.

For many years, I accepted my fate.

I no longer played with slingshots or climbed walls, and only wanted dolls—big dolls, small dolls, pretty dolls, ugly dolls, Chinese dolls, foreign dolls, borrowed dolls—if I did not have enough to play with.

Also, I would wash my face and brush my hair, finish my homework, and listen carefully to lectures on being a good girl. Then I would retreat quietly to my corner and play with the dolls.

Grandma was happy, saying, "My little girl is a girl after all. She returns to nature and controls her heart."

However, she did not notice that all my dolls were female ones.

I was trying to create a women's utopia.

No offense, male folks. Or I would not remember to go to the Tai Mountain[3] to worship the Sun.

The rising Sun beaming splendidly through the clouds often gives me hope and bursting energy.

And I am getting more and more disappointed in and ashamed of the Moon.

One of my neighbors told me a story about one of her colleagues, a doctor in a military hospital who insisted that someone else adopt her three-year-old son. The doctor had been ordered to leave on a military mission immediately after giving birth to the boy. She asked her parents to take care of him. After three years on the mission, she got the active boy back but found she was unable to handle the noise and mess. Out of desperation, she made such a decision.

Needless to say, everybody denounced the female doctor.

On the other hand, who could deny that she was true to herself? Actually, the most baffling moment is when women are arranged like flowers to receive sycophantic compliments. When women put smiles on their pretty faces, feeling satisfied and attractive, I feel my heart cringing. Then, I cannot help asking myself:

Who are you? Why are you here?

To be a celebrity? To seek the self? To be an observer? To drive away loneliness? To socialize to kill time? To search for the truth? To become wise? To be praised by others to satisfy vanity? To acquire a good reputation?

Compared to the female military doctor, well-dressed women who talk the "elegant talk" at ease may possess more materially but less intellectually. Burned with desires, women become mothers in all weathers, wives for all seasons, and daughters forever confined to the "peaceful scene"—each of them smiling in grace. But I know there are wounds deep down in their hearts. For this reason, I am baffled. Why do we need to manipulate things in such pretense? Our extra efforts wear us out, stripping us down to fleshless, soulless skeletons. We can neither please men nor become women.

I would prefer women's cries in bed at night when they are true to themselves.

Oh, when did women, including myself, become so pale and so vain, so superficial and so Machiavellian? Our loss of womanhood and selfhood makes even men inexpressibly disappointed.

Is there any value in being such women?

Of course, there are wonderful remarkable women whom I look up to and admire because they can help me purify my soul. Yet, in my broken heart, I feel sorrowful for them, because I know the fastest lonely walker has to slow down in hopes that the crowd behind will catch up.

"You must promise me not to put down girls!"

Says Daughter, word by word, pointing her index finger suddenly at my nose.

I can only answer with a bitter smile, and only in bitterness can I answer her question. My dear daughter, you think Mom is able to handle everything in the world. In fact, Mom is only a frail woman whose promise cannot protect you.

Mom once acted like you, pointing my finger at the nose of society and saying in anger the same thing you said. But each time I was the one who lost the battle.

Sometimes when she saw me unhappy, Grandma would do the chanting: "You have everything—food, clothes, and dolls. What else do you want, huh?"

I yelled back, "I don't want to be a girl!"

Grandma would laugh in response, "Don't be silly. . . ."

I said, "I want to play with slingshots and climb walls along with boys like a wild girl."

The smile immediately disappeared from Grandma's face.

Grandma, I am not blaming you, for it is useless. As a woman, I came to the world to suffer. I believe you went through the same painful ordeals. What I want to tell you then and now is: I have no desire for good food, exquisite silk and satin attires, or upscale home appliances. Nor do I want to be a celebrity to bring honor to my ancestors and family. What I want is a fine dwelling for my heart.

There was no road in the world.

What I respect the most are sisters who quest. Once at a workshop, I had spoken about interview techniques for five hours, but the question I received from my female audience was:

"What do you think of Chinese women's future?"

I could not look them in the eyes. All these women came from grassroots offices. They were good daughters, good wives, good mothers in their families, and excellent workers at their jobs. As women, they were living in painful weariness. This was why I did not have the heart to lie to them.

I tried to phrase what I meant to say in a humorous yet sarcastic tone, while nervously watching their responses. My heart was bleeding, but I did not want to break their hearts, hoping they would live a wonderful happy life free of the burden of thinking.

I was afraid to scare them, so I did not tell them, "I don't want to be a woman."

However, I regretted my elusiveness the minute I left the podium.

I regretted it to death.

Daughter finally crinkles into smiles.

It is now time to watch cartoons. She shuffles over, and, holding my hands in sweetness, nestles her head on my chest. At her age, cartoons matter more.

Indeed, the cartoon world is a nice one, a wonderful utopia.

I want to go to that world more than she does.

And never would I want to return.

NOTES

1. An outdoor group game where one hits the ground to turn the sides of picture cards. The more one turns, the more he/she collects. The winner is the one who collects the most.

2. Symbolizing *yang* and *yin*, the sun and the moon are often used to refer to male and female.

3. The Tai Mountain in Shandong Province symbolizes the highest point.

THREE AUTUMNAL
PHASES IN A DAY*

A thematic note:
   Three periods of autumn: Early, mid, and late. When they pass, savage winter is getting close in drumming hoofs.

At dawn when I should have gotten up, I sank instead into a strange reverie, in which a goddess shrouded in golden brightness told me, "Today, your city will go through all three periods of autumn."

I did not believe her. This fall, Beijing was experiencing an unseasonably nice weather.

Unlike the south that gradually moves out of heat to the warmth of fall in the midst of breezes and drizzles, the north, after seeing the first frost, becomes bitterly cold overnight. Ruthless weather starts its attacks like swords and spears cutting down violently. Then the whole world is wrapped in chilliness, a kind of cold that makes you depressed and hopeless. Worse, you are confined indoors. In about ten minutes, you will feel chills running down your spine. When they are biting your body from the brain to the toes, you are controlled by fear—unforgettable fear. These cold days always ruin the mood, making writing impossible. However, this year, though in its deep autumn months, had not seen any cold days. It was already late November, but the sun was still warm, and the golden fall only appeared on the edges of tree leaves. The weather forecast reported that it would be as warm as in the south, making cold-fearing Beijing people cheerful from the bottom of their hearts. Showering myself in the sunshine under the azure sky, I felt energized, working with double efficiency.

---

* Completed on January 3, 1996, the essay was first published in *Beijing wenxue* [Beijing Literature] 4 (1996).

So I told the goddess I refused to accept what she said. To be accurate, my refusal did not stem so much from disbelief as from unwillingness, hopelessness, or rejection. It might be, admittedly, fear.

But the goddess said sternly, "Humans never outsmart Nature in prediction."

I looked at her closely. An excitement surged in me—my God, guess who she is? The famous Miss Jane Eyre, who, I believed, was the strongest woman in British history. I remembered how she gave me great inspirations my juvenile years.

I became a little nervous but did not want to give in. Mumbling, I suggested, "Do you want to bet?"

Miss Jane burst into laughter and said seriously, "Okay, what do you have? Make a bet with them."

Rubbing my temples in a vain attempt to search for what I had, I realized that I was penniless, possessing no gold or silver except for my intellect—my virtual sanctuary for self-struggle. Out of helplessness, I uttered a sigh, grudgingly squeezing out these words through my clenched teeth: "If-I-lose, I-will-return-to-the-world-as-a-woman-again-in-the-next-life."

I was putting myself under a curse, wasn't I?

A

Shaking all over in nervousness, I started out of the house. Because of the bet I had made, I could not stop my eyes from stealing glimpses up at the sky every now and then.

It was not as bad as I had feared, however. At least, I felt the sun looked normal, rising inch by inch in its goldenness.

However, I had the shock of my life when I cast a glance at the ground. The streets looked odd with a thousand times more people than usual. All of them wore shoulder-long hair and skirts with heavy makeup—waxed eyebrows, shaded eyes, rosy cheeks, and bright lipstick. I didn't see anybody talking but heard nonstop droning in the air, a rather loud surrounding sound, as if thousands of people spoke at the same time.

I told myself to be careful.

Walking into my office, I saw a black envelope on my cherry desk. It was a fan letter from a reader I did not know. The opening sentence read:

"It's truly hard to imagine that a woman can reach such a higher order of thinking."

What does it mean? My jaws dropped open silently. I sneaked a look around quickly—fortunately, nobody was paying attention to me. My hands rushing to cover my mouth, I read on. The letter warmly complimented my essay "Women Don't Cry." The writer felt as if he had finally found a long-lost friend who had articulated his views thoroughly. He could not suppress the strong impulse to share his feelings in writing. To tell the truth, his letter touched me deeply. Tears rolling down my cheeks, I was happy that I had a heart-to-heart friend. My emotional response could be best described by a traditional saying—a learned person only writes for those who can see the meaning. Yet the beginning sentence in the letter upset me, making me almost wonder out loud:

"What about women, huh? Why can't women reach the high order of thinking?"

What the letter said was the most ridiculous thing I had ever heard; the funny part was that it was intended to be a sincere compliment, which had traveled thousands of miles to reach me via snail mail. I was entangled in endless reeling thoughts. Without careful deliberations, I passed on the letter to my partner, Mr. H.

Mr. H. was a nice handsome college-educated man from a well-educated family and appeared to be one of the best among countless outstanding men. His young mind seemed always receptive to cutting-edge ideas. But after reading the letter, Mr. H smiled slyly without comment. Tapping his long fingers on a newspaper, as if drumming his words into the soul, he said instead:

"Girls should never get a doctoral degree."

I asked, "Why?"

He mouthed bluntly, "When they get the degree, won't they become nitwits?"

"Whoa-whoa-whoa. . . ."

In the newspaper was a special report on Chinese female PhDs with photos of several women who looked pretty, smart, sweet, and lovely. I was thrown into a sudden shock at Mr. H's scathing comments. Sadness was wringing my heart—even such a young, progressive person was following the Confucian tradition faithfully. Then how many ambushes, gaps, swamps, and earthquakes are there on Chinese women's journey to liberation?

Miffed, I turned away to look out of the window but was terrified at the ghastly sight: Layers of layers of dark clouds blocked the sun tightly. On the ground, colorful flowers—chrysanthemums, roses, cannas, etc.—and fruit trees—banana, pear, and apple—were downcast in heavy dust, drooping their heads on hunched stems. All the trees—poplars, willows, scholar trees, mulberry trees, maple trees, ginkgo trees, pine trees, or cypresses—were under torture, their leaves mercilessly nibbled away by troops of yellow insects like the ghostly Gestapo splashing yellow color onto the trees in satisfied, evil-spirited, triumphal glees, howls, and dances.

"It takes only several dusks to end a sorrowful life"—yes, this was exactly how I felt.

The thought of what Miss Jane had told me made me shiver.

B

However, the weather changed for the better in the early afternoon—no whirling snows or boisterous winds—when I rode my bike on Second Ring Road to Beijing University.

Second Ring Road is the most beautiful highway in Beijing with attractive sceneries on both sides as a result of heavy investments. Because of what I had seen outside of my office window earlier, I watched around me carefully, looking to my left and right again and again at trees and flowers, including tiny ones, which, luckily, still kept their needle or flat shapes. The tree leaves, though yellowish now, were nonetheless displaying their lustrous surfaces under the support of the strong stems, giving no impression that they would fall off soon.

I felt teeny-weeny better now.

I was on my way to Beijing University for the "Women and Literature" session of the International Women's Conference. Nowadays, being a woman in China gives you some sort of sensation, as if you were the second daughter in the family who draws no attention on normal days but is suddenly promoted to a high status on important social occasions. I had attended several conferences on women and had published two books. In addition, I often received letters, phone calls, and even telegrams inviting me to write about women. But I did not want to write any more, "departing amidst the blistering windy rain"[1] of exhaustive coverage of women in newspapers and magazines, each abundant in rhetoric. This exuberating "women—women" talk should have boosted my self-esteem, but I did not know why—I was still unsatisfied and could not keep myself within "limits." Whenever I saw a woman in the street, I had the urge to ask her a question—in what way would the International Women's Conference affect your future?

Occupied with my thoughts, I saw a woman striding in front of me. Hurrying over, I was about to ask her the question. To my surprise, she/he started yelling at me:

"Look again! I am not a woman!"

I was stunned—it was not a woman! "But why are you wearing the skirt, huh?"

"Who says men cannot wear skirts?" He was bellowing in outrage as if he finally had found a way to let out anger. Standing in the middle of the sidewalk, he was bawling like a cock in fight, "Ugh, you women are allowed to wear male-style shirts, trousers, socks, and even A-shirts and boxers. Why don't you allow us to have our own way just for once? It's not fair. These days we men are treated so unfairly. Tell you what, we don't like it!"

"Okay-okay-okay, keep your skirt on, keep it!" Not wanting to get into a fight, I remounted on my bike, trying to flee from the scene. However, he chased after me.

"Open your eyes and have a good look. Isn't everybody in a skirt today?"

"Ah-ha," now it dawned on me—no wonder people were in skirts everywhere—men could take no more and were fighting back.

It would be an eventful autumn.

Upon entering the conference site, I saw many blond(e)s with blue or green eyes. Not all of them were females, though. There were a handful of males like a few decorative planets in the constellation. They were more conservative—still in tie and suit, looking formal for the conference. On the stage, Ms. Betty Friedan was speaking.

Ms. Friedan was not a nobody. Way past her middle age, her gray hair looked like silver locks casing a ring of light around her head, showing a spirit of lifelong work and pursuit. The elderly lady was a famous leader of the U.S. women's movement. Since the 1930s or 1940s, she had been an activist for American women's liberation. Her book, *The Feminine Mystique*, broke the path for the global feminist movement. In the West, the feminist movement started engaging profound inquiries and criticism, moving from appealing for gender equity and women's rights to challenging traditional ideologies in thinking modes, ethics, morals, cultures, philosophy, and the ultimate human concerns as well. Even the term feminism was replaced by the more accommodating term feminisms.[2] But in China, these changes, like the news coverage of astronauts being shuttled to the moon, seemed to bear little relevance to the majority of people who still tried to survive day by day with limited resources of food and clothing and to those males and females who were debating over skirts versus pants.

Well, not irrelevant anymore, I became relevant right away when Ms. Friedan called my name. I was woken up from the preoccupation of thoughts:

"Han Xiaohui, do you feel guilty?"

"I do," I responded as quickly and loudly as I could like a soldier answering the sergeant's call. I did feel guilty all the time. For instance, because I was attending this conference, I would not be able to get back home in time, so I was feeling guilty toward the man. Upon my arrival at home, I would dart hysterically into the kitchen, the "University of Home Economics," where I studied in the "Department of Domestic Physics" offering courses in scrubbing pots and pans, washing dishes, cleaning the floor. . . .

"Yes, I know—I know," Ms. Friedan broke in, "the gentlemen attending the same conference, however, have completely different stories to tell. They are achievers, who can enter the house in self-pride ingrained into each cell of their bodies—from the chest to the tips of the hair and to the toes; their cockiness seems to demand their wives feed food into their mouths. I know . . . I know how you feel. This has been my experience and all American women's. Every woman has gone through it."

"But do you think you are through? Are you sure?"

Ms. Betty Friedan shrugged, spreading her hands.

Lost and mortified, I walked out of the conference site to Lake Wuming. Good Lord, what a horrible sight! When did the beautiful jade-green water suddenly become sewage sludge? There were only twenty or thirty daylilies in the water, hopelessly curling up their darkened sick leaves and drooping over the hunched stems as if in silent praying. Reeds, withered and dry, did not whisper autumnal solaces anymore, posturing like desperate homeless senile people frozen in ice storms with their hands up, pleading with Nature for mercy. The ginkgo trees, no longer poetical beauties, were suddenly banging in strange explosive sounds, showering little berries like raindrops as if shedding tears.

In distress, one of Li Qingzhao's poems crossed my mind:

> The scent of red lotus fades: the jade mat feels autumnal.
> Gently loosening the silk gown,
> I board the orchid boat alone.
> Who's sending a gilded message in the clouds?
> When the migrating geese bring the word
> The moon will be full in the western chamber.[3]

Generation after generation of students, including myself, studied and memorized "Yi Jian Mei" as a classic love poem. But today why did I feel the poem was not about love anymore? Why didn't I even believe the word "love" could synthesize the feelings of such a talented historical woman—feelings that "go straight to the heart, just when they brim in the eyes"?[4]

Her brilliant poetry and her projection of the self, as well as every aspect of her life, went well beyond traditional bounds. She outshined many men. Wasn't this the worst, unforgivable sin a woman could ever commit? Was it possible that the old tradition restricting all women for centuries showed favoritism to Li Qingzhao alone? Deceive me not. I did not believe it anymore. At these concurrent thoughts, the "autumnal" effect in Li Yi'an's[5] poem and the word "autumn" in Miss Jane's remarks sounded horrifying now, haunting like weeping, wailing ghosts awakened by the autumn amid endless grief and hate.

I began to feel the horror: Is it true that the autumn will end today?

Cupping my hands together and lowering my head, I could not help mumbling prayers to all gods and goddesses: please . . . don't . . .

C

The beeper in my purse went off like an ambulance siren.

It was a message from Li Xiaoyu, a famous poet and a friend of mine,[6] who asked me to arrive at the Italian Embassy at five o'clock to meet some Italian female attendees to the International Women's Conference who wanted to talk to Chinese women intellectuals. But I did not think I could make it because I had already committed to the China People's Broadcasting Station's live show "8:30 Tonight" to talk about my career as a female correspondent—also a special arrangement in response to the conference. Xiaoyu did not let me go, saying that I would still have three hours to kill between the meeting with the Italian women and the radio show. No-no-no, I repeated, because I had yet to prepare for the show. Besides, honestly, what could I talk about? I could not suppress my sad, embittered "reactionary" feeling, with "tears streaming down the face."[7] Was I an unsalvageable sheer lunatic? Xiaoyu did not care about how I felt at this moment. She said, "I'll see you there," and hung up.

My watch read 4:30 now. I took a deep breath and dashed frantically out into the street. Risking my life in traffic to hail a cab, I eventually opened the door of one that was still running. Getting in the cab, I saw the big and tall driver in male-style clothes who asked in a surprisingly soft voice, "Where to?" Cautious because of the lesson I had from the early afternoon encounter, I kept my mouth shut except for giving the direction, without looking at the driver in the face. However, she broke into laughter and told me she was a woman. Now I started to look at her—wow, she was in pants. Right afterward, I could not help telling her about my earlier encounter with the man. Tickled by my story, she was laughing hard, shaking herself back and forth. I took the opportunity to ask her:

"It seems you are a feminist, or you wouldn't be wearing pants."

"Ahem," clearing her throat, she started complaining in a strong northern accent, "What a boxing game [over rights][8] between men and women! I don't care. It's a lot of trouble. You see? In the morning I was asked to wear a skirt, and in the afternoon, I was required to change into pants. It's almost five o'clock now. After giving you this ride, I'll run to pick up my kid and prepare supper. Soon after washing the pans and dishes, I'll be back to driving on the street again to catch some more business."

Troubled, I asked, "How about your husband? Doesn't he do anything?"

She replied in a tone of anger, "The big master? How can he lower himself to sweep the floor with a broom? Wouldn't people gossip and jeer at him like crazy? We women from the country are way more behind than you liberated city women!"

I was dumbfounded.

It was getting dark now. The dark clouds were casting lower and lower, and the high buildings began looking dusky. In the east of the city landscape were many skyscrapers blocking the sky and shading the streets, where grand hotels were entertaining extravagant banquets. The glaring neon lights blinded me—I could not tell whether or not autumn still kept its presence on the tips of trees. Fortunately, I was not late. But no sooner had I seated myself in breathlessness than three Italian women sauntered in. I learned from the introduction that one was a scholar, another one a teacher, and still another one a community social worker. All of them were researchers in women's studies.

I talked about my essay "Ranking Women," which had been triggered by a question from a gentleman, who, after dividing women into five types—family women, career women, sentimental women, erotic women, and luxury-seeking women, asked me which type I would consider the best. I told the Italian women that 99.999 percent of Chinese men held "family women" as the best type. They simply wanted women to stay at home. In other words, even if women worked outside the home, their hearts were required to remain at home in service for their husbands. But today's Chinese women, particularly educated women, had their own ideas. No longer believing that men were women's only world, they thought that women should have their own careers, feelings, life goals, and enjoyments. Of course, the obstacles remained as big as high mountains. Women were victimized in brutal manners. For example, they were forced to leave home or have divorces or were battered to the extent that their faces were permanently damaged and their bodies disabled. Chastised by society, some battered women died in the streets without anybody to take care of their corpses. At these words, however, I remembered to add, "The future is brilliant. . . . The road is torturous."[9] Immediately, I followed up, saying that compared to the brutal old society [before 1949], however, we had made tremendous, tremendous progress.

The three Italian women seemed fascinated. Their eyebrows, like the two hands on the clock pointing alternately to a quarter past nine, ten past ten, or twenty past eight, were sometimes even, sometimes raised, and sometimes arched. Their faces took different shapes as well—sometimes long, sometimes round, and sometimes triangular. They asked me many interesting yet odd questions: Do you write for men or for women? Is it men or women that you think can transform the world . . . ? To them, I asked an even stranger question: Do you want to be a man or a woman?

Unfortunately, time was ticking away fast, alarming me again—I had to go now. So, there I was, apologizing for taking off so abruptly, nodding my head like a chicken pecking at food. Immediately afterward, I leaped out of the building like a panther and, the instant I was in the cab, urged the driver to hurry up. God knew why I was still clear-minded and remembered to take a look at the trees on both sides. There were still some leaves on the poplar trees, but they looked like cooked greens, softened and curled up, near death.

In such a hurry, I did not notice whether the driver was in a skirt or pants.

D

My mind seemed too muddled up to remember what happened next.

I only remembered that I was in front of the microphone, feeling like a little mouse under the gripping paw of a lion. In a hard struggle, I summoned my blood, flesh, strength, spirit, soul, as well as my sense of faith, honesty, and responsibility to manage an eloquent talk on the show. I sounded calm, confident, full of self-respect and self-dignity, and energetic in high revolutionary spirits, sending the message that I fully enjoyed a blissful life as a career woman. I repeated thirty-eight times "How bright and brave they [women] look, shouldering five-foot rifles / On the parade ground lit up by the first gleams of day."[10] For at least forty-eight times, I recited, "With a mere snap of the fingers / We can clasp the moon in the Ninth

Heaven / And seize the turtles deep down in the Five Seas."[11] I repeated resonantly, at least eighty-four times, "Be resolute, fear no sacrifice, and surmount every difficulty to win victory."[12] I ended my speech by reading "While the prospects are bright, the road has twists and turns" at least 168 times. After the show, the hostess told me that my talk was such a success the audience responded enthusiastically. Many people also wrote letters to tell me that "their hearts swelled with emotions," "their blood was invigorated," and "their eyes were filled with tears." However, deep in my heart, what abysmal shame and insurmountable chagrin I felt!

I remembered that I spurted out of the studio to make a phone call home. On the other end of the line, my daughter, Liang Siyan, a fifth-grader in the Shijia Hutong Elementary School in Beijing, was complaining vigorously:

"Mama, it's late. Why aren't you back yet? I have a test tomorrow, and the teacher wanted parents to help prepare for it. Why don't you care about me . . . ?"

I fell instantly into an icy pit. In worry and anxiety, my heart felt unpleasantly fiery hot, making me sweat all over. I darted out of the radio station building.

This I remembered clearly—when I got to Chang'an Street, I started to cry.

Needless to explain why.

Now falling dead leaves, like leaflets, were swirling up and down all over the street, echoing the miserable gnawing world—"ye-ye-ah—ah-whoa-whoa." The poplar trees, willow trees, Chinese scholar trees, mulberry trees, maple trees, gingko trees, silk trees, parasol trees, as well as pine trees and cypresses, were watching their leaves falling off from the top and turning the color from yellow to odd bright golden. Thousands of gleaming transparent leaves, like homeless ghosts, were howling, spinning, bouncing, and quivering. Halfway up to the space, they paused, hesitated, and struggled, fighting the forces of gravity to stay away from the ground. Once they touched the ground, however, they were immediately turned into dazzling white snowflakes. Suddenly, the dreadful snow came to cover everything—the streets, roofs, the world, the universe, the Heaven, the earth, the body, the face, and the heart.

I had not seen such heavy snow before in my life, which, by no means noiseless, was roaring and whistling like the winter winds. It was not falling down to the ground in layers but shooting up yards high; it was not freezing cold but burning hot. It was not projecting images of classic beauties, such as Zhao Feiyan, Wang Zhaojun, or Yang Yuhuan, whose "single mirthful glance imparts hundreds of allurements,"[13] but the images of women warriors on the battlefield like Hua Mulan, Mu Guiying, and Qiujin. It was no snow in the traditional sense but snow in a transformed modern sense with white blazing flames rocketing miles high like powerful human arms extended upward to the sky.

The street was empty, no one in sight.

It truly was the end of autumn.

NOTES

1. From the poem "Farewell at Xie Pavilion" by Xu Hun (Hsu Hun) in the Tang Dynasty.

2. Han uses two Chinese terms *nüquan zhuyi* (women's power/right-ism) and *nüxing zhuyi* (female gender-ism). For the cultural connotations of these two terms, please see "Introduction." Han does not read English, so she may think that there are two different terms in mainstream Western feminism. For readability and with respect for the development of Western feminism, the translator decided to use "feminism" to refer to *nüquan zhuyi*, and "feminisms" *nüxing zhuyi* in this context, instead of using "womanism" because of its specific Afro-American connotations.

3. Translation adopted from *Women Writers of Traditional China: An Anthology of Poetry and Criticism*, edited by Kang-I Sun Chang and Haun Saussy (Stanford, CA: Stanford University Press, 1999), 92.

4. Ibid. The order of the line is altered in this context.

5. Li Qingzhao's studio name.

6. For Li Xiaoyu's poems, see *Women of the Red Plain: An Anthology of Contemporary Chinese Women's Poetry*, translated by Julia Lin (New York: Penguin Books, 1993), 56–62.

7. From "Jiang Cheng Zi," a poem by Su Shi (Su Dongpo) in the Song Dynasty.

8. Han uses *quan* as a pun for both "rights" and "fists."

9. Mao Zedong, "On the Chungking Negotiations."

10. From Mao Zedong's poem "Qi Jue: Militia Women Inscription on a Photograph."

11. From Mao Zedong's poem "Shui Diao Ge Tou: Re-Ascending the Jinggang Mountain."

12. From "The Foolish Old Man Who Removed the Mountains," by Mao Zedong, *Selected Works*, vol. III.

13. From the poem "Song of Endless Sorrow," by Bai Juyi (Po Chu-I) in the Tang Dynasty.

WOMEN DON'T CRY

It is painful that women are unable to cry. The ugly world often tries to kill you with its monstrous claws. You want to sever them with your sword but find you are too frail. Now you feel your blood vessels pounding in explosive blows. You would rather die than suffer the humiliation, but you do not have the heart to leave your sweet little daughter behind. Looking at the gems of her black eyes, you feel your heart churning in grief. How badly you want to cry! At least crying could express your anger, your will, and your protest. Although you know that it is the last resort, crying nonetheless could release you from a heavy emotional burden. After crying, you could borrow energy and power from thunder and lightning.

All women's tears do not indicate weakness.

However, something must have gone wrong because you are unable to cry. How come?

Even though your sadness is so gnawing it could gather high-rising tides from all the rivers and lakes on earth, even though your throat is swollen to the size of all the mountains on earth combined, you are still unable to burst into tears. Like the morning dew, the more you want tears, the less they come.

You are helpless, hopeless. The only thing you can do is kneel down like your ancestors and pray to God, telling him that you have tried to cry and you have pleaded for tears. But God wants to punish you by further drying up the springs in your heart and throwing you into flames of fire.

In the fire, your beautiful shiny hair is burned into strings strangling you more and more as they form tight knots, your eyes like two bloody holes. Seeing the whole world on fire, you cannot help screaming in gut-wrenching desperation:

"Is it my fault? What did I do that violated the Commandments?"

75

At this moment, you envy the women who are able to cry!

They shed tears like strands of pearls described beautifully in poems: "Dropping random notes on the musical instrument / Tears stream down like pearls large and small"; or "the moon is full on the vast sea, a tear on the pearl. / On Blue Mountain the sun warms, a smoke issues from the jade"[1]; or

> Tears on the pillow,
> Raindrops on the bamboo curtain,
> Separated by the window,
> Till the morn they drip in echo.

Amid women's chanting weeps, the whole world melts in empathy. Swept by the breeze to the sky, crying women ride on beautiful rainbows. At this sight, men are deeply touched. Voluntarily, they stretch out their arms that are as strong and as long as the Great Wall to hold the women close to their broad chests, even if they are unable to create a wonderland for these women.

Men love women in tears, which are the source of their own heroic spirit.

Unfortunately, you don't cry, though you know weeping and sobbing move men. Suffering has changed you—no longer a fool that cherishes dreams and illusions. You cry no more and, unfortunately, fall out of men's favor. Thinking of you as his dangerous enemy, Big Brother Wu[2] is like a lion on full alert, staring at you and ready to pounce upon you. While he cannot take good care of his own business, he taps his fingers with ease to make your life miserable. This world order has been determined since the ancient times. It doesn't matter what you do, you can never afford to look down on men. You must cry to them, or they will mark you as "insensitive."

This consequence is not hard to imagine because the Sun is still the Sun even if he shines no more.

Out of exigency, you must consider a serious issue—how inconvenient is it that a woman is unable to cry?

You can see the picture in your mind's eye. On the boundless plains stretching as far as the eye can see, two women, one in red and the other in white, are about to take a journey on their saddled steeds. They are equal in age, physical build, life goals, timing, and risk factors. The only difference is that the one in red is able to cry. Summoned by her tears, a caravan of knights come on their horses to pave the road for her, a troop of bodyguards come to watch her front and back, and other men come to umbrella her from the rain and cheer her with songs. The woman in red enjoys a smooth ride with comfort and safety as well as joyful romance, reaching her destination with ease. The other woman who does not cry, however, has to start the journey alone, vulnerably exposed to the ugliness, brutality, and barbarity of the unsympathetic nature entrapping her with monstrous beasts and poisonous serpents, barbarians and freebooters, and swamps and murky, muddy rivers. Showing no mercy, Nature pours down rain to whip her and shoots forth thunders to deafen her. . . . When the woman in white finally reaches her destination, she is deeply wounded all over. Her clothes are in shreds, her hair wild, and her heart in profound sorrow. The horse, her only loyal company on the journey, is all bones and blood.

Because she does not cry, she is fated to undergo such distressful hardship. The miserable journey is only one of thousands of adversities in her life.

A woman who does not cry is destined to suffer because she deprives herself of opportunities for men to spoil her, to protect her, and to hold up the sky for her. There is no place where she can hide herself, no backups, and no time for self-consolation, let alone a confidant to whom she can share love and hate from her heart. To her, the world is a sea of evolving misery. When can she eventually find a peaceful land for herself?

On the other hand, it is good that women do not cry.

You can pose upright. You do not hunch over. You can look at people directly in the eyes, tell the truth, do things you believe in, and treat others with honesty and compassion. You can also sing and laugh freely in delight, put on beautiful clothes and makeup at your own will, and enjoy freedom in all sorts of activities—swimming, hiking, reading, writing, and watching movies. You will never, ever, experience the humiliation of kowtowing.

In your eyes, the Sun is gold, the Moon jade, the sky genuine diamond, and the Earth jadeite. This way, women maintain the true self that embraces mountains, rivers, woods, plains, towns, villages, flowers, trees, planets, and the universe in their natural forms, true forms to be kept by both men and women who are true to themselves.

Needless to say, the human, unlike plant life, experiences various emotions, the heart like an active volcano provoked by love and hate, sweet memories and bitter wrongs, happiness and sorrow, ups and downs, separations and reunions. Being no saints, women surely have their moments of weakness and weariness. At these moments, they run back home to lick their wounds alone through humming, dancing, cooking, sewing, or having a good cry—all by themselves. Their cry, though not sonorous enough to shake the earth, brings back their self-control. If we believe that men should hold back their tears, then women should not shed their tears to plead for help. Life is not easy for either men or women. Takakura [a Japanese movie star] once said, "As men, we have to hold back a lot." But women have to hold back even more. . . .

We, women whose lives depend on literary writing, must thank God for his endowment.

When we are unable to cry, we pick up the pen to give free rein to our reeling thoughts, letting them rise like ocean tides or pour down like waterfalls amidst thunder and lightning. This is the utmost joy of life.

As a matter of fact, all women are able to cry, but they cry differently in practice, in manner, in purpose, and in value. In short, I want to say that women who uphold honesty and self-dignity are the most attractive and beautiful.

NOTES

1. From the poem "the Patterned Lute" by Li Sangyin (812?–858) in the late Tang Dynasty. Translation adopted from www.dpo.uab.edu/~yangzw/lishy1.html#1.5 (accessed July 23, 2007).

2. A character in *Shui Hu Zhuan* (The Water Margin).

IV

HU XIN

Hu Xin (Hu Qing) was born in 1945 in Nanchang City, Jiangxi Province. Among all the writers in this collection, Hu was the only one who was a college student before the Cultural Revolution began. Unfortunately, her college career was interrupted in 1968 when Mao's administration sent secondary and college students to receive reeducation from peasants in the countryside (*shang shan xia xiang*). Hu was sent to teach in the Xintain Village Elementary School about one hundred miles away from Jingdezhen, the ancient porcelain capital and the only city with bus service. On the bumpy dirt road, young Hu Xin burst into tears out of fear and sadness, which would accompany her hard life in the following years. The only city girl with a college education, she soon became the target of the predatory school principal. When he failed in his attempts at sexual assault, he organized school-wide meetings and mobilized students to denounce Hu Xin's "bourgeois" lifestyle. She recalls: "My warm tears in the cold wind were counting the miserable days in those years." When Hu Xin sent out her first fiction, "Four Women of Forty," for publication, she changed her given name from Qing (pure and clear) to Xin (hardship), a move cynically reminiscent of a period of her life controlled by the state machine and reflective of her view on Chinese women's life in general, a life out of their own control, a life hard and sorrowful.

"Four Women of Forty" won her first literary prize in 1983—the China Best Fiction Award—and was introduced to English readers in 1991.[1] Since then, Hu has won many national and regional awards, including the Northeastern Literary Award (1991) for *The Rain of Roses* and the China Contemporary Women's Literary Award (1998 and 2003).

Hu is now a professor of Chinese in the Department of Chinese Language and Literature and the director of the Center for Film and Television

Arts at Nanchang University. Apart from her teaching and research, Hu has published nineteen novels and short stories, such as *Selected Works by Hu Xin* (four volumes), *Here is Spring Water, The Black Sun on Earth, The Rain of Roses* (adapted to a thirty-episode television series), and *Tales of the Porcelain Capital*, as well as essay collections, *Women's Eyes, My View on Women,* and *Women's Footprints of Pain.* Hu's additional works include biographies: *The Romance between Chiang Jingguo and Zhang Yaruo, Biography of Anna C. Chennault,* and *Eileen Chang: the Last Witness of Aristocracy.*

The essays in this anthology are chosen from her collection *Women's Eyes.* Although the essays share similar concerns about gender inequality with the other writers in this anthology, Hu's essays emphasize basic human values, regardless of the gender, and they celebrate female/male difference in contrast to the tradition of using difference to oppress. Hu's concept of human equality speaks to a notion of feminism that asks women not to blame men and men not to blame their female counterparts but, instead, to acknowledge how difference is historically used as a weapon against both sexes.

This notion of the equal human in Hu's writing is especially important to the understanding of post-Mao Chinese feminist philosophy and discourse. In the West, a person is born a human, and hence a woman unarguably a human. Due to this contractual agreement on women's human status, Western mainstream feminism was late in recognizing women's rights as human rights until it was challenged by studies of race, class, and Third World women (also see Apodaca; Okin; Riddell-Dixon). The Chinese tradition, however, holds that humans are developed *not born.* The Chinese notion of human embodies two facets—the physical person and the cultured person. The physical existence does not necessarily entail a person's human status, because every person is not born a human, and all humans are not born equal. Those who have received education and understand human relations are humans who can serve in offices. The uneducated ones who lack the understanding of human relations are not considered humans and are excluded from public offices. The life goal of a Chinese is to become a human above other humans (*ren shang ren*), particularly that of a Chinese male. This tradition naturally deprives women, who were born to a lower status than men, of human status and human rights as well.[2] By reflecting on women's human status, Hu questions not only women's social position, but also their human rights.

Based on this notion of human equality, Hu subsequently urges us to reach consciousness through "a rebellion against patriarchy but not a return to matriarchy." Her writing honors the acceptance of the female life experience as an awakening to both males and females without the compromise of female identity, which should be recognized as the strength of being a human different from men. Hu's wisdom and maturity in being a woman, a mother, and a writer portrays her as an example for a different human with a profound understanding of human equality.

NOTES

1. *The Serenity of Whiteness*, translated by Zhu Hong (New York: Ballantine Books, 1991), 158–87.

2. For a full analysis of the Chinese concept of human, see Hui Wu, "The Paradigm of Margaret Cavendish: Reading Women's Alternative Rhetorics in a Global Context."

WOMEN'S FOOTPRINTS OF PAIN

Preface for the Reprint of "Four Women of Forty"

In 1983, my first novelette "Four Women of Forty" enabled me to set foot in the door to the sacred hall of literature. In the opening, I asked, "Why do women have their own holiday?" At that time, I was writing more with uncertainty and eagerness than with analytical insight.

More than ten years afterward, I finished ten books in addition to teaching. I have never been a celebrity nor sunk into obscurity. In retrospect, I have devoted all my efforts to the quest of women's independence, searching, seeking, and repeating the effort, yet without much success. I do not think people should worry about women writing about women. Nor do I forget I am a woman when writing about women, considering traditional society still holds women in discrimination and contempt. I have written about famous women, ordinary women, senior revolutionary women, traditional women with deep secrets, working-class women, and even petty city women. What I have written about the most, of course, are educated career women, whose lives are the most familiar to me because I am one of them.

Examining women's gender consciousness, I once ventured a definition—"You must know you are a woman. Women, like men, are human beings. But women are humans different from men." I was aware that this kind of reasoning sounded strangely circular. But I am still wondering to what extent women can achieve their autonomy independent of men because they are limited by the reality that the human race is either female or male. I have yet to think this through. I am still unsure if my fictional female characters, including myself, have advanced or obscured women's consciousness, which, like I have said, is unclear and complicated in the first place. I still cherish the hope that all our quests will not result in vain attempts but in the enhancement of women's consciousness. This is why the characters in my fiction, though perhaps not perfectly crafted, are born from my heart and true observations.

Writings about career in relation to romantic love, family, and relationships are often simplistically considered lacking the grandeur of heroism. What they convey, however, are true meanings of life, a life imperfect in many ways. I still believe that women's happiness springs from motherhood, and their sorrow from the pursuit of romantic love. Different from fatherhood, motherhood does not only mean "physical changes in the body" but represents the strongest chain of life as well, transforming an ordinary passage of life into selfless, profound human compassions and emotions. The pain, dignity, and responsibility of becoming a mother are infused into her blood and heart. Just as Lu Xun notices, motherhood is inborn, and wifehood inculcated. For many years, love constitutes not only a special aspect of a woman's life but also the only, or the major, way to realize her dreams. Admittedly, these views may be a little overemphasized or even out of date, but they echo my view that love bespeaks women's faith and totem as well as their tragic limitations. And a female novelist cannot create the beautiful and the true unless she has the courage to face her own limitations.

The setting of my fiction is Jiangxi, where one sees red soil and touches pure white clay. My works never repeat the cliché often used to dignify my home province—"a place of splendid things and heavenly treasures as well as outstanding men and blessed soil," because, I believe, it reflects a biased history of male pride. Instead, I write from an alternative point of view to trace women's footprints of pain in the same soil. Red soil naturally imparts the impression of infertility and thus, poverty, but women living on the red soil do make sincere and wholehearted contributions. When combined with water and tempered in fire, white clay atop the hills can make the finest porcelain, which, however, is also the most fragile due to its delicate and fine nature. In this aspect, this land seems to hold some philosophy of life—radiant bright red soil and immaculate serene white clay can be materialized only on a land that cherishes beautiful dreams. Women are born dreamers. I wish when they finish reading my works, they can relate to the beautiful land of Jiangxi.

According to Chinese customs, a fiftieth anniversary enjoys a great celebration. Now the literary circle has started a new fashion to celebrate the tenth anniversary of a writer's debut. My ten years, however, have only witnessed peacefulness and quietness—I have not fallen into the unknown, nor has my ego swelled to the point where I would forget who I am. My experience may prove a Chinese saying that a lucky person only lives a Nature-endowed life.[1]

NOTE

1. For readability, a brief acknowledgment in the end is omitted.

A PINK HUMOR*

As a label, "little woman" is fondly favored by men and accepted by women as well, even some educated women thinkers. But does the acceptance signify a revival or a decline of women's consciousness? Does it mean that women's values are enhanced spirally to a higher level or weakened in a different manner? Is it exaggeration to cover up possible humiliation or humor to offset a serious tone?

The "little woman" projects the image of a little bird being petted in dependency—an attraction irresistibly arousing male empathy and fantasy. However, dependency does not mean relying on the male but acknowledging the woman's self, as well as conversing playfully with confidence in the male-dominated world, despite her comparatively smaller physical build.

The "little woman" thinks, speaks, and writes about trivial daily routines that seem so common, ordinary, and insignificant that she is criticized for limiting herself to the delivery room, dining room, bedroom, or clinic waiting room and being obsessed with little sensational details of sorrow, happiness, or affections. Nevertheless, who has the right to say that only fighting in wars is important, and bearing children is unimportant? The space given to the "little woman" is, in truth, narrow and confined with little headroom. The question is: Who has ever given the woman a sky spacious enough for her to fly around or a borderless plain for her to roam over? Otherwise, wouldn't women's efforts in fighting for public positions and economic independence count as fusses?

"Little woman" may be intended as a harmless contrast to another label—"superwoman," which both strong and frail women try to avoid being

---

* First published in *Jinan Daily* in 1997.

associated with, because it is almost equivalent to a "woman looter," or, at best, an emotionless "iron girl" without a trace of femininity. At the same time, however, isn't it true that both men and women deeply respect and admire Iron Woman [Margaret] Thatcher? Aren't they fascinated when they read about women warriors governing gangsters or a powerful madam managing interior affairs for a captain of bandits? These women are still females whose only differences lie in their extraordinary personalities and abilities as a result of unusual experiences and opportunities. If strong women wanted to change themselves back to little birds, they would have to break off their strong wings. If little women want dependency, they will have to become tamed, land-bound hens. Therefore, many women know that our rejection of the label "superwoman" is an action against disparaging womanhood.

Does this rejection mean that only the "little woman" can keep womanhood? Is a woman born naturally or made by the thousand-year-old male-centered tradition and culture? Doesn't civilization mean the realization of patriarchy, as Beauvoir reminds us? But from the bottom of his heart, the modern man also expresses deep concerns, "We are under more stress than women." Why so? Because a male-centered culture serves as a double-edged sword. On the one hand, it gives men a sense of superiority; on the other hand, it puts them under huge pressure because they want to show that they are stronger and smarter than women in hopes of winning women's respect and worship—the more, the better. However, the fact is that men are no smarter than women, and for this very reason, males disapprove of strong, smart women living under the same roof. Therefore, "little woman" as a label bespeaks some male expectation of the female, reflecting male taste and aesthetics. From this point of view, a woman who wants to develop femininity in order to please men has to compromise her own sensibility and sensations.

For a long time, lost was the woman who persistently and painstakingly looked for the manly man without realizing that she was actually seeking dependency. Admittedly, having a man to rely on can possibly lead to happiness, but history tells a different story: In reality, women, not men, have always been protectors and guardians for the human race. Almost all heroes in literature, from princes in antiquity fleeing from their enemies to the male characters in *Legend of the Tianyun Mountain*[1] and *Half of Man is Woman*,[2] rise above their misfortunes because women render their love altruistically. If the man and the woman in any of these stories reversed their roles, would he do the same for her as she has done for him? Contemporary "little women" know better. To explore their own path, they shed no tears, laughing and speaking in their own voices.

Thinking of Socrates' famous saying that the wisest man knows that he knows nothing, I add that the wisest woman knows that she is a "little woman," because, as a standup comic on this year's CCTV Spring Festival Show notes, "small things hold the best and the most beautiful in a condensed form."

NOTES

1. A novel by Lu Yanzhou.
2. A novel by Zhang Xianliang, translated by Martha Avery (New York: Norton, 1988).

MY VIEW ON WOMEN*

Wwhat is woman? This is an old yet a new topic forever under discussion.

It doesn't matter whether or not the woman was created by God from man's rib or made of earth by Nu Wa.[1] It doesn't matter whether the saying that "women's bones and flesh are as fluid as water" serves as a compliment or as a stigma when the wording changes to "women's nature is like water that always flows downhill." It doesn't matter whether the harmony theory posits that men are rivers and women sailboats, or that men are trees and women vines. Nor does it matter whether the negative theory suggests that women are not soil and men not the soil crate, or that women are not the moon and men not the sun. Whatever these views are, they manifest that since the ancient times, both men and women have been incessantly grappling with the subject of woman in participation or in observation, though in different tones and manners—from serious to humorous, or from thoughtful to playful.

How favorable and yet unfavorable this situation is for women!

People sometimes discuss men rationally and search for the manly man, but the topic of man has never dominated our fascination. Nor do men have the need because in a society centering on male interests and willpower, they do not have to rally around a pro-male flag. Men can keep their pace with pride to stride toward the future in triumph, without being bothered by the criticism of "deteriorated manhood."

From this perspective, the concern about women embodies both a patriarchal tradition and the revolt against it, symbolizing the sensation in

---

*Written in December 1990 and first published in *Literary Forum*, 1991.

the male gaze cast downward at women and the low self-esteem women show consciously or unconsciously. But more important, it also symbolizes the souls of awakened women in persistent quest.

Women had built a prosperous matriarchy in the primitive society, where they held significant ruling positions both in economic production and human reproduction. However, along with socioeconomic development and labor divisions in later civilizations, patriarchy came into existence, resulting in "the overthrow of motherly right," or "the *world-historic defeat of the female sex.*"[2]

Social development should have led to historical advancement, but the male ego swelled out of control. Perhaps out of the instinct to protect patriarchy, it debased females to mere instruments of labor, reproduction, and entertainment, excluding them from public activities. Women did not count as humans. With a long history of feudalism, China designed and developed meticulous, deep-rooted conventions for "non-human" women to observe. The bride's wedding cry[3] materialized patriarchy that had replaced matriarchy. Various wedding rituals served as prayers for the blessing to have sons. The wedding song has long prescribed inequality between a son and a daughter at birth. It sings:

> So he bears a son,
> And puts him to sleep upon a bed,
> Clothes him in robes,
> Gives him a jade scepter to play with.
> . . .
> Then he bears a daughter,
> And puts her upon the ground,
> Clothes her in swaddling clothes,
> Gives her a loom-whorl to play with.[4]

This feudal brutality is further written into the rites: "An unmarried woman obeys the father. Married to her husband, the woman obeys the oldest son after her husband's death. She must be a follower who should never initiate any independent action."[5] All these customs, on the one hand, symbolize the burden of tradition upon women and, on the other, seem to indicate women's resignation to their long historical tragedy.

Women, however, do not surrender silently in despair. Their literature is an example. In *Searching for Her Self in the Lost Half*, Chen Huifen points out, "When history relentlessly excluded women from all public activities, women 'preserved' their identities through their own literature. When women's emancipation came of age and advanced, women discovered themselves in their literature." Though not yet predominant, Chinese women's literature, particularly that of emerging contemporary writers, forcefully expanded boundaries to explore women's consciousness and values.

In 1983, my first novelette, "Four Women of Forty,"[6] enabled me to set foot in the door to women's literature. Since then, eight years have passed. In the opening of my first fiction, I have raised the question of why women have their own holiday; I have quoted [Henry Wadsworth] Longfellow—"Into each life some rain must fall, / Some days must be dark and dreary"—to open my 1990 novel *The Rain of Roses.* So far, I have created a fair amount of female characters. However, I do not know whether I have enhanced or obscured women's consciousness and values that are unclear and complex in the first place.

What is women's consciousness? You must know you are a woman. Women, like men, are human beings. But women are humans different from men. This reasoning seems to entrap us in a strange circle, which, I hope, will not see itself in repetition but in spiral elevation.

Being an independent human being is an essential step for women. Nevertheless, how hard it is to stop the habitual and natural dependence on men and to conquer the sense of female inferiority! Besides women, the rest of the human race is men. So even if women are independent, to what extent can they achieve full independence? I think breaking down the old and new conventions symbolizes women's independence. This means that there will be no mandate on how women should behave or speak, what attires and makeup they must wear, what personality or temperament they must develop, and how they should think and feel. What disgusts me the most is the requirement that "a female behave like a woman." What upsets me the most is men's reprimand of women for not behaving like a female and women's fear of losing femininity. What outrages me the most is the comment of literary critics that women's writing has lost its feminine characteristics! Why can't people forget that we are merely females? Yes, women are different from men. But aren't men different from one another? Aren't humans different from one another, and so are women? When humans' fingerprints differ, how can their personalities be identical? Personalities are indeed diverse and complex. When men and women are judged, both masculinity and exquisiteness should be regarded as beauty, so should candidness and reservation as well as toughness and delicacy. . . . Why should there be a universal standard for feminine beauty? As for literary works, they are artistic creations after all. Why should they be judged in relation to the writer's sex? When males design women's fashions, should people worry that their products lose masculinity? In this regard, unless they change their sex, women who cut themselves loose from conventions should not cause any astonishment.

Nevertheless, women are humans different from men! They experience, or at lease yearn for, motherhood, which is different from fatherhood. Mothering not only represents "physical changes in the body" and the chain of life but also a meaningful passage to a life full of noble sensations. The pain a mother has gone through, the dignity, and the responsibility are infused into her blood and heart. Reproduction means life conceived from "love," whether it is true or false, sensible or irrational. Balzac writes that "man's life is fame, woman's life is love."[7] To women, romantic love stands for faith and totem, but also tragic limitations. For these reasons, there is grief in "Love Must Not Be Forgotten," sorrow in "Where Did I Miss You," sadness in "Don't Talk about Love," agonizing numbness in "Too Lazy to Divorce," and more. Most women writers and critics believe that the action of "Leaving the Eden" reflects women's awakened consciousness,[8] but it is impossible for women to take the action, except women in fiction. In reality, no women can, not even women writers and critics!

Love is intertwined with women's consciousness and values. When writing "Four Women of Forty," I knew clearly, "career, ideals, struggle, love, marriage, family . . . [are] hard for women." But with "[q]uestions at every turn, Where are the answers?"[9] All the women characters—Lingling who lives a good life without realizing it, Yehyun who experiences two divorces and three marriages, Shuhua whose life is buried in daily routines, and Liu Qing who searches for pure and noble love—dream about careers and ideals. Some of them live in happiness because of realized dreams, while others live in sorrow as a result of vain efforts. I became uncertain by the time I was writing *The Rain of Roses*. In this novel, the peaceful small neighborhood once dominated by interests in literature and education is shattered by the tempestuous torrents of economic reform. The seven well-educated sisters, the ordinary sweet young maidens, as well as "the pauper's beloved daughter," are besieged by various new moral values, particularly those of romantic love and marriage, battling and adjusting themselves among conflicts between sensibility and passion, between the soul and flesh, and between ethics and lusts. Even successful career women in the novel are floating around or drowning themselves in the sea of romantic love. Of course, life is not all about love, but one cannot live without love. At the same time, however, yearning for romantic love does not mean depending on the male. Social problems are not caused by emotional upheavals of awakened women or by changes disturbing "the orderly world" women have once lived in. After all, they represent the rhythms of women's life pursuits. The problem is that the seven sisters in *The Rain of Roses* may well be the last generation of educated women. This prediction is neither exaggeration nor groundless worry. Soon to emerge will be a generation of uneducated women—numerous other seven sisters, ten sisters, or undocumented daughters of "families on the run from birth control authorities."[10] Their personal development will be greatly impaired as a result of abandonment, discrimination, and illiteracy.

It is admirable that today's educated young women are often free spirits. However, the promotion of free-spirited young female characters in the works of some emerging young women writers may be misleading. A free spirit devoid of life experience is weak to the core because only a lived life, not a young age, can endow women with free spirits. When in the open, the heart of a free-spirited young woman is often vulnerable because she still lives in the same old world as that of her mother. Maybe the young heart needs to be armored with abstinence, which is not chastity developed and reinforced by patriarchy to imprison and yoke women. Crushing chastity defined by patriarchy, women may want to keep the armor, not abandon it, to gain independence.

Meanwhile, to overcome the mentality of female inferiority, we must face the male world sensibly. Don't men try hard to keep their values as well? Don't they also yearn for love, love that is noble and transcendental? In this regard, there is not much difference between men and women. We are all human.

Therefore, blaming men for women's suffering and pain may indicate an effort to veil low self-esteem and incapability, just like men blaming women for toppling empires already in self-destruction.

Strong women and frail women are normal phenomena because as opposites, the mighty and the weak always exist in equilibrium. They reveal themselves everywhere—in personality, capability, positions in the family and society, and career successes or failures. The obsession with love and power in the historical stories of Queen Cleopatra and Empress Dowager Cixi only give women doubts about independence, for inside an elderly woman's body, still beating forcefully is her wounded heart, where profound values of womanhood can be found. As Nietzsche points out, not unreasonably, "[w]ill is the manner of men; willingness that of women."[11]

A woman's loving heart embraces not only romantic love but also boundless, profound, and altruistic love.

Therefore, women's consciousness means a rebellion against patriarchy but not a return to matriarchy. It is a long historical river in which women and men sail together toward a bright future.

This essay is not an attempt to establish a theory but to express my random thoughts.

It is emancipation for any woman if she is allowed to express her opinions and act according to her own observations.

This is perhaps the meaning of this essay.

NOTES

1. The Chinese creation goddess. For a complete story, see kongming.net/novel/kma/nuwa.php.

2. Frederick Engels, *The Origin of Family, Private Property and State* (New York: Pathfinder, 1972), 68. The sentence is modified to fit the context. The italics are in the English original.

3. Tradition encourages the bride to cry out loud to show that she is unwilling to leave her parents for her husband's family.

4. Translation adopted from *The Book of Songs*, translated by Arthur Waley (New York: Grove/Atlantic, 1996), 162–63.

5. From *Guliang Zhuan*, or *Chun Qiu Guliang Zhuan* (*The Guliang Chronicle*), one of the thirteen classics in Confucianism, which is said to be written by Guliang Chi in the Spring and Autumn Period (841–476 B.C.E).

6. In Zhu Hong, *The Serenity of Whiteness: Stories by and About Women in Contemporary China*, 158–87.

7. Translation adopted from Simone de Beauvoir's *The Second Sex*, 669.

8. The quoted are titles of women's fiction.

9. Hu Xin, "Four Women of Forty," 187.

10. Even though China has been carrying out the one-couple-one-birth policy since the early 1970s, a family in the country still wants to have a son to carry on the family name and support the aging parents. When the first two births in a family are daughters and the wife is pregnant again in hopes of having a son, she is often on the run, sometimes accompanied by her family, from a mandated abortion.

11. *The Gay Science*, www.pitt.edu/~wbcurry/nietzsche.html.

V

LU XING'ER

Born in 1949, Lu Xing'er died of cancer in Shanghai in 2004 after she finished her last collection of short stories, *Women in Deep Waters*, and her last novel, *The Pain*. Lu served as a professional writer with the Shanghai Writers' Association and a member of the China Writers' Association.

Growing up under Mao, Lu was tremendously influenced by Soviet Russian and Chinese socialist literatures that encouraged young citizens to be utterly devoted to the Communist Party's causes. She dreamed of becoming a heroic figure as those created by Nikolay Ostrovsky in his fictionalized autobiography *How the Steel Was Tempered* (1932). In 1968, Lu answered Mao Zedong's call with eagerness and passion to move to Beidahuang, a remote rural area in extreme poverty in northeast China. She was full of energy and idealism in the first three years, but life in the impoverished countryside was far less romantic than she read about and imagined. The poverty and hardships gradually disillusioned her in terms of ideology, life goals, values, and beliefs.

Lu's literary work was very much of her time and reflected her thinking and experiences. Her first short story, "Cattle Horns," was published in 1974, and her second short story, "Red Maple Leaves," was published in 1976. These stories narrated about young people like her on the farm and promoted Mao's revolutionary cause. But this theme discontinued in 1978 after the Cultural Revolution ended. Lu became disillusioned about Mao's socialist revolution and went to college to study dramatic writing at the China Central University of Theatre Arts in Beijing. She paid more attention to "love" in relationships and among people. When she was a sophomore, her short story "Seeds" was published in *Fiction Quarterly* (now *Youth Literature*). Collaborating with Chen Kexiong, her colleague and later her husband, she published several novels, such as *The Ocean in My Heart* and *We Have Grown Up*, and short stories, "A Female Postal Worker in the Green Uniform," "The Half of the World," "The Snow Has Stopped," "Oh, Chrysanthemums in the Distance," and "I Love You—Wild Lilies." In the meantime, she published three novels of her own—*Constructing Beauty, Oh, Blue Bird*, and *To My Unborn Child*.

After her college graduation in 1982, Lu published over twenty novels, more than ten collections of short stories, and seven essay collections. During the following years, Lu was more and more intrigued by women's lives and the problems they faced daily, particularly after her divorce. One of her translated novelettes, "Under One Roof," was based on a true story of an award-winning high school teacher whose husband had an affair for years. Due to the lack of additional housing for split families[1] and society's rejection of a divorced woman, and for the sake of her children, the teacher had no choice but to stay in the marriage. "The Sun Is Not Out Today" is about women who undergo mandated abortions, and "The One and the Other" about a young woman who is romantically involved with a married man.[2]

Incorporating her own life experiences into her writing, Lu crafted female characters "to demonstrate that they live in a struggle under the burden of traditional values" (Q. Lu 366). Her female characters reflect her own battles, her own confusion, and frustration. Lu has learned, from her own marriage and men she knew, that men, bound by tradition, esteem their own social status, institutional positions, and power more than love. Mostly cowards and hypocrites, men would never sacrifice their own interests for women they claim to love. It was not until after her divorce, which forced her to raise her son without a stable living space and to solve other daily life problems alone, that Lu began to examine her selfhood and to understand who she was. From her self-exploration, she began to examine gender and women, particularly career women. It was also during this period that she started to rethink the value of the female individual. She concluded, "The loss of marriage has brought my self back, which is so important to my life. Establishing a family may not be difficult, but finding one's self is, because many women often lose themselves and do not know how to position themselves in the family."

The essays in this book are selected from her collection *Women Are Not Born* published in 1996. Similar to Hu Xin, Lu Xing'er also emphasizes human equality. However, Lu extends the human value to the value of individuality that Chinese women are often taught to lose for the interests of others. Perhaps Lu was less optimistic than Bi Shumin or Hu Xin, when she reveals her poignant observation of the disconnect between the reality-as-we-want-it and reality-as-it-is. Although she seems to hope that if she could solve her female characters' dilemmas, she could solve hers and other women's, she sends a hopeless message that the realities of real lives could not be remedied even by imaginations. Despite her hopelessness, Lu still wants to raise women's awareness of how they have been duped into believing that they have gained freedom from admittance into the public sphere, when in reality they have only doubled their responsibilities, a standpoint echoed by Zhang Kangkang's essays in this anthology and shared by Chinese feminist critics.[3]

NOTES

1. See Shu Ting's essays in this anthology for the housing problems single women once faced.

2. These three pieces are in *The Serenity of Whiteness: Stories by and about Women in Contemporary China*, translated by Zhu Hong (New York: Ballantine Books, 1991).

3. See the "Introduction." Also see Xiaojiang Li's "Economic Reform and the Awakening of Chinese Women's Collective Consciousness" and Hui Wu's "The Alternative Feminist Discourse of Post-Mao Chinese Writers."

WOMEN'S "SAMENESS"
AND "DIFFERENCE"

Women often complain that being a woman is truly wearisome. I can relate to the complaint. Women are worn out not only physically, but also mentally and emotionally.

Since we were young girls, we have learned the truth: Women are half the sky, and women and men are the same. As slogans, these words roll out from the tips of our tongues; we felt proud and inspired. We transformed these words into actions to become as capable and smart as men—there were "iron girl troops," "Eighth of March[1] conductor groups," "women pilots," and so on. In all walks of life, women performed as well as men, to say the least, and did whatever men were able to do. It was a common belief that women advanced at the same pace as that of men. The catchphrase "men and women are the same" was reinforced repeatedly for so many years that it became a universally accepted worldview. The phrase was also supposed to signify a historical change—Chinese women's liberation.

However, I beg to differ.

Things in the world are different because of their different natures. The motto, "men and women are the same," in fact, only sets requirements on women without asking men to do what women do—bringing up children with patience, taking care of house chores without complaints, and caring for the parents of both families with devotion. Indeed, this slogan has encouraged women to make as many public contributions as men do. At the same time, however, women have done many things that men do not do. In this respect, the slogan of "sameness" is biased because it requires females to be both woman and man; it fools women into taking in more responsibilities. In reality, women and men are not the same.

Following the decades—long belief in "sameness," things and situations have changed along with economic reforms. Men have also "liberated" themselves in terms of desires and needs, rephrasing at the same time what they demand from women. No longer emphasizing "sameness," they have created a new campaign cry—"females must behave like women to be attractive." In essence, the cry indicates the male demand that women return to tradition to be different from men. It is even applauded as a symbol of Chinese women's progress.

Yet I do not agree with this idea either.

When "sameness" is emphasized, women and men are actually not the same. When "difference" is emphasized, women still must work as much as men, in addition to domestic responsibilities. No wonder women are worn out by such a hard, wearisome life. If they want to shield themselves from male contempt, they must keep the "sameness," and if they want to appeal to men's sexual desires, they must maintain the "difference." These demands are too unfair, too much for women. Besides, utter sameness and difference is almost impossible to accomplish all at once through women's efforts alone without certain favorable economic conditions. This is a hard mission to accomplish. Indeed, the slogan—"men and women are the same"—has allowed women chances to elevate their social and economic positions. The cry, "men and women are different," to some degree, offers some way for women to enhance their integrity. The problem is that women's liberation in the name of "sameness" and women's "progress" through "difference" both subject women to men's requirements. Why doesn't male-dominated society also require men to liberate themselves from the traditional thinking to make progress at the same time?

I believe that behind the catchwords—"sameness" and "difference"—there are some deep-rooted problems.

NOTES

1. March 8 is Women's Day.

ON "FEMININITY"

For many years, women's magazines have been flooded with fastidious consultation on how to enhance femininity, how to dress, how to apply cosmetics, how to tone the body, and so on and so forth. It is understandable that this kind of advice balances the aftermath of poverty and political suppression in the past. When bound by poverty and censorship, we were unable to dream about better lives and diverse lifestyles. Today, a better economy and higher life standards allow us to develop femininity, which, unfortunately, has been turned into a hot topic in extreme terms. As a result, "superwomen" are looked down upon as non-women. The overemphasis on "femininity" forces a large number of women to remain "virtuous wives and good mothers," while maintaining the momentum of their successful careers. After describing their career successes, writings about "superwomen" have never failed to add that these women have fully observed feminine virtues for fear that the public would doubt if they still belong to the attractive female sex. At the same time, women who are desperate to demonstrate their female sexual appeal are popular and promoted, feeling satisfactions everywhere they go. These women of "femininity" brag about their "conquests" of successful men. And in response, some magazines report "talented guys with pretty girls" in exhaustive detail, particularly the romances and marriages of actresses famous for their impeccable "femininity." By promoting "femininity," these magazines indeed serve as their own advertisements. Under their influence, some women trade themselves, perhaps unconsciously, as commodities with men for social status and material life. A close examination reveals that the promotion of "femininity" merely encourages women to please men. These ceaseless lectures on "femininity" make me sad.

What is "femininity"? "Heaven's law and Earth's decree"[1] (*tianjing diyi*) seem to have prescribed its characteristics for women—they must be

101

pretty, soft-spoken, submissive, and exquisite. A close look at the law and decree shows instead that the components of "femininity" are developed by human beings according to male taste and demands. For a long time, I have been writing a series of fiction titled *Born a Woman*. I think that all women's problems stem from the fundamental belief that females are born women and are different from men. If such is the case, then a woman is born feminine, anyway. Then why do we need to overstress and promote "femininity?" Doing so only means that society still restrains women from equality and requires them to meet its gender criteria by satisfying men's psychological and physiological needs, as well as other demands. Evidently, it will take a long time, not overnight, for society and men to become sensible before they eventually withdraw their demands—a bleak prospect to them indeed. Yet bleaker is the fact that some women identify male demands as their own life goals to pursue "femininity," worrying whether or not they measure up to men's tastes and likes. These women excessively mind men's protection and love, which they dearly hope to obtain. Unfortunately, this susceptibility, no matter admitted or not, is women's vulnerability, the source of their misery and sorrow. They must closely follow the male standard of "femininity," which in turn becomes their own goal for self-improvement. Even intelligent and competitive strong women are afraid of being blamed for being unfeminine or undesirable. It seems that women can hardly move themselves out of the male shadow, no matter how strong they are. For this reason, they have difficulties developing autonomous individuality and the consciousness of independence.

As women, we need to consider the same issue as men—the human issue—human integrity, human quality, human morale, human responsibility, human life, human sensation, and human thought. All these are "humanity," not merely "femininity." Only when a woman becomes such a noble human with a pure soul will she develop "femininity" naturally.

NOTES

1. Referring to Confucian doctrines.

ONE IS NOT BORN A WOMAN

For many years, I have been writing fiction about women. I write about their sorrows and joys, separations and reunions,[1] love and hate. A title that might sum up all my stories could be: One is born a woman.

I like this title, concise and precise, revealing the essence of my writing. Indeed, a woman seems born with hardships and problems—congenital, predetermined, destined, inevitable hardships and problems impossible to overcome and resolve. One day when rethinking about the women in my stories and their innermost feelings, I suddenly realized that even though their difficulties and dilemmas differed in manner and subtlety, deep down they were similar—they kept seeing themselves so repeatedly as women that they played the traditional role naturally. Society, history, and culture have long prescribed the role, function, purpose, desire, pursuit, happiness, and misery for women. On a life stage built on traditional conventions, no matter how hard and how persistently they try, women seem unable to feel equal and be independent individuals. Once resuming the traditional gender role, even a talented woman with tremendous career successes is not able to maintain her selfhood, just like an ordinary woman without ambitions. To illustrate this "impossibility," I wrote incessantly about women in fiction and essays that amounted to nearly a million words,[2] and with so much inspiration and energy. The enormous landscape made by the million words, however, did not show me a way out of the "impossibility."

I wrote about how women studiously pursued their dreams without compromise, though painfully aware of the bias that came with age.[3] I wrote about how women daringly endured humiliations as a "third person"[4] rather than give up love. I wrote about how women remained unmarried to seek freedom, but ended up with alienated souls. I wrote about how women quietly swallowed insults from their unfaithful husbands to save face for their families. I wrote about how great, yet how pathetic, women were when they had lost their selfhood in consequence of their entire dedication to their husbands and children. I wrote about how women overdosed their children with love to cover up their distorted lives and personalities as a result of disappointing marriages. I wrote about how infertile women were tortured by guilt and driven to the brink of insanity under social pressure. I wrote about how women were embittered when awaiting mandatory abortions on the cold benches outside the surgery room.[5] I wrote about how insidiously women's exhausting, hectic lives smothered their basic human desires. I also wrote about how some women tried to appeal to men sexually for material benefits but had to live with empty souls . . . and so forth. Writing about women, I fully understood their feelings and standpoints. And in response, I sighed heavily from within in sadness. I wrote and wrote, without explanations, without answers. Maybe life was life—there was no explanation. But how much I wanted to find a definite answer!

Then, a statement in a book sprang to my mind: "One is not born a woman!" All of a sudden, I saw the light as if I had woken up from a long, long deep sleep that lasted thousands of years. Yes, why don't we strike back with a counterargument? Woman is not born! Though it is still vague, I seem to have found the answer.

NOTES

1. Under Mao, most people did not have the freedom to choose where they wanted to live or work. Jobs were assigned by the government or one's institute. If a couple happened to be working in different regions, they were allowed a thirty-day (fifteen days for each) family leave (*tanqing jia*) per year to visit each other. In most cases, children lived with the mother. Because the chances to change jobs were slim, this kind of separation could last until retirement.

2. The royalty received by the writer depends on the amount of words in the first print. Therefore, most Chinese writers remember how many words they have written. The number of words, in addition to the amount of published books, is also used to judge a writer's productivity.

3. Age discrimination in China creates many problems for women. See "Introduction" for more explanations.

4. The term (*disanzhe*) stands for a person who is involved in a love affair with a married person. In most cases, it is a moral censure on the single woman in love with a married man, while the married man is often assumed to be seduced by the woman and deemed free of guilt.

5. Lu is referring to her fiction "The Sun Is Not Out Today."

WOMEN AND THE CRISIS

In recent years, I have been thinking about women's issues and written about them in a fiction series. I plan to continue writing about these issues in the future. Indeed, since ancient times, woman has never failed to be a topic involving prolonged, heated discussions. I am sure that women will continue to be talked about, in depth and forever. However, women's situation and future will see few fundamental changes, despite so much writing, thinking, and discussing.

I said "fundamental," not superficial.

At a superficial glance, Chinese women seem emancipated, particularly urban women who have been working outside the home to make their own living along with men under seemingly equal conditions. Nevertheless, making her own living does not automatically lead to a woman's independence and liberation. Many other issues, such as values, mindset, physiological build, and habitude, still restrain the woman. As a result, she is unable to reposition herself. Many of today's women, though no longer socially enslaved, still regard themselves as dependents of men, sometimes out of willingness, sometimes out of habit, and sometimes out of lack of option. The only equity they have acquired is a job or a career, which oddly makes them more wearied and stressed. As for women's social positions, there is little improvement. In other words, females seem to be born women. In the past, I tried to seek a way to independence and self-reliance for the characters in my fiction, or, in a candid term, for myself. I once believed that as long as a woman had established herself successfully in a career, the world would change its attitude and honor her with a higher social status, a better life, better everything. But many things in evidence proved that my wishes represented only the goodwill on women's part. Life, of course, cannot be calculated with a math formula. Indeed, competent, strong, and successful women can now hold up their heads in public. But, on the other hand, how much does a strong woman have to take when she is gossiped about or jeered at as a "superwoman?" This is such an unfriendly term without appreciation and respect, a term of ridicule and derogation used to describe women who are considered disagreeably non-woman. What oddity this term connotes! It is equally odd that the public accepts it, though not yet openly promoting it. Consequently, women with great achievements often experience odd sensations of low self-esteem. A positive term has thus oddly turned into a negative one, a term whose "honor" and "glory" all females are shying away from. Odder still, even if the term may mean an honor or compliment, it hurts a woman's image.

This is truly odd!

But after thinking it over, I do not feel odd anymore. Some men feel uncomfortable around strong women because they believe these women have destroyed the harmony of the male-centered world. No wonder men have acted up. Aren't newspapers and magazines good examples? There is endless news coverage of single women in graduate programs who fail to find husbands and spinsters in their late twenties in personal ads. To their credit, some of the reports are well-intended attempts to promote pub-lic awareness of potential social problems. But repeatedly reporting how females fail in relationships harms women's public image and, as a result, attaches negative connotations to "capable women" and "strong women." Nowadays, morals and values have indeed changed, and so have men's stan-dards of women. They now want women to be attractive, gentle, sociable, and cheerful. They do not want women to be capable and hardworking. As a result, women who are considered not pretty, not tender, and not sociable are doomed. Oftentimes, when men look at a strong woman, they think to themselves: When the woman becomes a wife, she had better return to the happy home and hearth. The woman should devote herself wholeheartedly to her child and husband without complaints and make the home clean and cheerful. When her husband comes back from work, he can enjoy a nice dinner in the warmth of home. In men's eyes, this type of virtuous wife is the "true woman." Furthermore, she should be able to dance with him, ap-preciate the music he likes, and entertain him with interesting conversations. A wife so devoted to the family is the most desirable woman, the perfect woman. This male "design" may be a perfect arrangement. But the problem is: Where do we find this perfect world? The greedy man often has an insa-tiable appetite with regard to women. On the one hand, he makes his wife thoroughly devoted to him. On the other hand, when his wife loses herself in the long, busy routine of homemaking to make him happy, he invents new excuses—"our life goals are no longer the same," "she and I do not share interests anymore," "I cannot stand talking to her anymore," etc., etc. It does not matter how wonderful a woman is, society never recognizes and accepts her. She is bound to anguish and frustration.

A woman is not allowed to be either a strong woman or a "womanly" woman. What an unfortunate dilemma! Whatever she does or says, she is always at fault, as if she were arraigned on a criminal charge in the midst of the crowd's sneers and scoffs. Because of my writing projects, I have interviewed many women in different walks of life. Listening to them, I heard the question they were all pondering in their hearts: What life should a woman live after all? She is torn apart by the dilemma in a crisis. She wants a career to empower herself, and she wants society to recognize her as a womanly woman as well. In such internal conflicts, it seems right that she should esteem the latter more—being a "true woman" to live a practical life of love with a family and a husband. After all, she is a woman who is supposed to compromise submissively. However, even though the compromise may lead to happiness, it oftentimes entails undesirable results, or worse, tragedies.

I feel deeply that many women, including myself, are faced with a dilemma—how to fit into such a society of constant moral changes and keep our selfhood intact?

In order to help the female characters in my fiction rise above the crisis, I tried various options, none of which seemed to work. In other words, none of my characters could transcend the crisis, as if they had moved in cycles, for this is a male world after all. For thousands of years, women have been leading their lives through men's eyes, and male perspectives have gradually become the criteria women use to judge themselves. As a matter of fact, conversations about women are comfortably centered on male interests. So far, of all the theories on women, is there a single one anchored in women's equality? In *The Second Sex*, Beauvoir quoted Balzac saying, "In all the codes of so-called civilized nations, man has written the laws that ranged woman's destiny under this blood epigraph: '*Væ victis*! Woe to the weak!'"[1]

What a comment! We are reminded that the reason for her crisis is that the woman places herself in the position of the "defendant," pleading guilty to the charge against her "weakness" with no chance of defense. Indeed, she is conscientiously engaged in self-criticism, yielding to the accusation that her weakness is the cause for global misfortunes. She tries to be a perfect woman in every possible way to please men. However, in spite of her efforts, it is impossible to be "perfect." The efforts on her part can hardly make the world less complicated and life less problematic. In contrast, as the ruler of the world, the man seldom engages himself in self-reflection or self-criticism. [Bernard] Shaw points out, "The American white relegates the black to the rank of shoeshine boy; and he concludes from this that the black is good for nothing but shining shoes."[2] Under the similar oppression, women are forced to assume a subordinate position and develop physical and mental dependency. This mentality is hard to change, even if women are aware of all these wrongful accusations. They are frustrated.

From this perspective, only when a woman changes her mindset—ceasing to view herself through men's eyes—can she form her individuality and establish her own evaluative criteria for her sex.

Women in truth possess many natural talents. They are brilliant, strong, and full of feminine tenderness and motherly affections, particularly Chinese women who are diligent, hardworking, warmhearted, and caring. Day in and day out, they participate in the same productive activities as fully as men on the same terms under the same conditions. Meanwhile, they conscientiously and exclusively shoulder domestic responsibilities of childcare and house chores. They are overworked to be the best, to live, to work, to achieve something, and to make contributions. Being so competent, outstanding, and remarkable, they should not endure any oppressive restrictions. After all, doesn't society want women to be wonderful, perfect, and competent? But when women meet its demands, what does society reward them in return? Compared to men, women have lower social status with fewer opportunities to develop and realize themselves. When they are in the process of self-development and self-fulfillment, they must make extra efforts, overcome extra difficulties, and undergo extra hardships. With so many extra accomplishments, women indeed should be proud of themselves.

As such, women must be confident with high self-esteem and full self-recognition. As human beings, women and men should be equal. The world belongs to both sexes, of which neither can be missing. I think that we, women, must understand ourselves, respect ourselves, and promote ourselves from this standpoint so that we can explore ourselves without narrow-mindedness, emancipate ourselves from oppression and degradation, and transcend accusations. This way, we will eventually realize ourselves as true human beings to enjoy individuality and liberty. Compared with a profession, a title, or a diploma, individuality and liberty are more difficult and yet more important to obtain. While in theory we are able to accomplish the former without any barriers, obstacles do exist everywhere. And many times we hinder ourselves, since tradition has confined us for too long and brainwashed us too thoroughly. Nevertheless, only through professional and educational achievements can a woman empower herself, protect herself, and defend herself, ultimately enabled to control her destiny without frustration and to overcome the crisis and obstacles.

For all these reasons, women must encourage, praise, and promote one another to enhance their self-esteem and self-dignity. Women must feel equally heroic and accomplished as men. In fact, in addition to the unique, great motherhood responsible for human reproduction, the other contributions virtuous women have made in all aspects of life are invaluable and immeasurable.

Talking about women in such a way, I truly feel that all feminisms, feminist standpoints, and all theories on women have come into existence just because women have never shared the world equally with men. Women need their own epistemology to mobilize themselves. Of course, fighting against men may make men develop new theories to control women more strictly. On the other hand, it seems that the more radical the theories are, the stronger women's appeals are and the more liberated they are. Only when there is no doctrine to lecture women and no need to stress women's standpoint—that is, when women stand up as human beings equally and naturally without the support of theory—will women be fully liberated as independent individuals.

Maybe I am a little off track,[3] but when a person encounters a dilemma or a crisis, deep visionary thoughts can often help him/her gain a good understanding of the current situation. Since a woman is often accused of being shortsighted and shallow, speaking out her futuristic views brings her no harm but benefits.

NOTES

1. Translated by H. M. Parshley (New York: Alfred A. Knopf, 1971), 256.

2. Quoted in Simone de Beauvoir, *The Second Sex*, xxiv.

3. A comment must be made here. The translation of this sentence is faithful to the original. Sounding apologetic, this transitional sentence indicates a very much gender-based response from a woman writer. Lu could imagine potential criticisms of her for exaggerating women's crisis and gender inequality. This form of writing echoes exactly what she has criticized—the "impossibility" to transcend the crisis.

I

112   Shu Ting

elusive imagery and

disappointment a

Between

which late

by Shu T

are a

A

SHU

S hu Ting was born in 1952 in Xiamen, Fujiang Province, across the Taiwan gulf. Growing up under the ideological control of Mao's administration, Shu still managed to read books, some of which were criticized as bourgeois or poisonous. In 1965, she was accused of reading "unhealthy" world literature—translated works by Balzac, Mark Twain, Hugo, and Tolstoy. In her own defense, Shu said, "But there are no more Chinese books left for me to read." When she was seventeen in 1969, Shu was sent by the government to do farming in an isolated mountainous area. Through the separation from her family in "exile" (in her own words) and hard labor, Shu could relate to the impoverished, hard-working farmers. At the same time, she knew that young lives of her generation were being sacrificed for the government. To reflect on the lives of her own and the people around her, Shu wrote poems in her letters to her friends, wherein she criticized the censorship and expressed desire for freedom of speech.

In 1972, she was transferred back to Xiamen, and in 1975, she started working in a factory. Meanwhile, Shu never stopped writing poems, which she exchanged with her friends, Bei Dao, Mang Ke, and Gu Cheng, even though there was little hope to publish these literary pieces on freedom, humanity, and individuality.

Finally, in 1979 after the Cultural Revolution, Shu Ting's poem "Ode to the Oak Tree" was published in *Today* magazine, a journal cofounded by dissident poets Bei Dao and Mang Ke, and then reappeared in *Poetry Periodical*. This poem expressed her strong sense of being an independent human equal to men. In post-Mao literature, "Ode to the Oak Tree" not only pioneered the new poetry, which emphasized humanity and human issues, but also foreshadowed the "misty school of poetry" led by Bei Dao, who used

linguistic ambiguity to express desires for freedom and
ideological control.

1979 and 1982, Shu Ting published over a hundred poems,
appeared in collections such as *Double-Pole Boat*, *Selected Poems*
ing and Gu Cheng, and *The Singing Iris*. Many of Shu Ting's poems
vailable in English, including *Shu Ting: Selected Poems*, *Selected Poems:*
Authorized Collection, *Mist of My Heart: Selected Poems of Shu Ting*, and
individual pieces. In the early 1990s, Shu Ting started to publish essays. Her
collections include *Sky-High Aspirations* and *Collection of Shu Ting's Essays*.

Shu Ting has been active in global cultural exchanges. In 1986, she
was invited to speak at the International Conference on Chinese Literature
in San Francisco. Between May 1996 and April 1997, she was an artist
in residence at the Germany Science and Literature Exchange Center in
Berlin. She is a member of the China Writers' Association and the vice
president of the Fujian Writers' Association. Shu Ting has won many literary awards—for example, the First China New Poetry Award to Young
and Middle-Aged Writers, the China Best Poetry Award, and the New Era
Women Writers' Award.

Shu Ting believes that she belongs to "the third generation of Chinese
poets" emerging after the Cultural Revolution. She says, "Undergoing a
peculiar historical period makes us responsive to the history, mission, and
values of our country. Understanding the burden, we are more conscious of
social problems, collectivity, and humanity" in comparison to the younger
generation of poets, whose works center more on individuality, perplexity,
restlessness, and mysteriousness to transcend cultural bounds (Q. Lu 673).

The essays in this collection present Shu Ting's critical insight into
patriarchy and tradition that are suppressive of women. The change in her
writing from poetry to essays gives Shu Ting an additional venue and more
literary space to discuss women and women's literature through their gender
roles and daily life. From historical women who made sacrifices for men
to modern choiceless women, Shu Ting tells of a restrictive sexist society
where women encounter much more problems in life than men.

Although Shu Ting claims that she is not a feminist, her essays,
nonetheless, express a progressive feminist standpoint that a woman should
have the freedom to make life decisions independent of her prescribed roles.
Ironically, Shu's own married life and the lives of the women tell different
stories—women's lives are defined by their sex. By telling the real-life
stories in nonfiction—her dialogue with her husband and the singled-out
single women—Shu exposes the sexist nature of society. Perhaps to her,
being a feminist means to transcend gender and to be a human who has the

right and freedom to choose. When deprived of these rights, women are deprived of *human* rights. Shu's message prompts readers to imagine that a woman's right to make decisions about her own life should be the ultimate goal of feminism.

Furthermore, from the viewpoint of genre, some of Shu's essays adopted poetry writing skills, a move that deviates from traditional prose writing. Playful with the language and style, Shu demonstrates her adroitness as both a poet and an essayist. For example, "A Mirror of One's Own" in this anthology sounds incoherent in textual development and elusive in meaning if read according to the traditional standard of prose. However, readers perhaps cannot take at face value Shu's essays. As an established poet and essayist, Shu's choice may be intentional. Maybe she wants to transform the traditional essay by blending in poetry-writing techniques, or maybe she wants to demonstrate her skills and sensitivity as special features of women's writing, features that are impossible for male writers to obtain. Regardless of her intention, Shu's writing reflects her desire for creative freedom. This move not only challenges the male-dominated prose convention but also turns the sexist contempt for women's literature upon itself: Women writers are able to employ their unique insights to do whatever they want in writing once they have become masters of the convention. Shu's clever move in essay writing will be further illustrated by the next writer in this anthology—Zhang Kangkang.

SHADOW OF THE CHASTE TEMPLE*

On an evening, my husband was reading the newspaper, while I was editing my manuscript.

All of a sudden, waving the newspaper in excitement, he urged me to read a human interest report. I never read personal stories in newspapers and am satisfied with my ignorance. But he started to read out loud. At his insistence, I had to put aside the manuscript.

The story was about a country girl who married at eighteen. A year after her marriage, her husband fell in love with another woman and eloped. Abandoned and without hearing a word from her husband, the woman kept her chastity and painstakingly raised her husband's four younger brothers, despite all the difficulties. Now all of her brothers-in-law graduated from college. Two of them even earned master's degrees.

I commented, "Country people marry young. Her in-laws must have been only forty-some then."

Pointing his forefinger at the newspaper, Husband answered, "Yes, her father-in-law died ten years after her marriage, and her mother-in-law has been in poor health ever since."

Then, I told him that the four younger brothers-in-law were not orphans and should have been raised by their own healthy parents. The woman had no reason to sacrifice and victimize herself.

"Maybe the academic diligence of the brothers-in-law touched her deeply. Maybe she wanted each of them to move upward on the social ladder," Husband replied.

---

* From *Du bian wanglai* [Reader-Editor Correspondence] 3 (1996): 31.

Even if this were the case, the older brothers must have been several years senior of the younger ones. The first one who graduated from college should have had a job to support his younger brothers. How can an educated professional (no, actually four) let the woman endure all the hardships by herself year after year?

Yet Husband tried to defend the story again, saying, "This woman was so determined that no one could change her mind."

What if her four brothers-in-law had not graduated from college and did not have good jobs? What if they had stayed in the country, farmed, got married young, lived a peasant life with wives and children, or even wasted their lives by gambling and stealing? In the latter scenario, would she be honored as a female saint? What's more, she was not yet forty years old, according to the news story. After she had made so many contributions, why didn't anyone think of helping such a virtuous woman to establish her own family? How on earth was she able to change her life under the spotlight? It was reported that her brothers-in-law remained filial to her after they were married. However, in a society where even an urban career woman finds it difficulty expressing her opinions on the matters of her husband and her child, how could the families of her brothers-in-law accept this country woman who, in her senior age and without her own income, would have to take turns living with each of them and depend on them financially? Is this scenario possible, even if the wives of her brothers-in-law were kind and their children understood family obligations?

Furthermore, is a senior citizen's good life solely about sufficient clothing and food?

Last year, I visited the China's Temple for Women in the memorial park of She County, Anhui Province, and saw the stories of chaste and honorable women, who added footnotes to and expanded *Lives of Exemplary Women*.[1] For example, an eighteen-year-old unmarried girl tried to breastfeed her baby brother after their mother died. Nature's heart was moved and filled her breasts with rich milk. When in his adulthood, her brother won first place in the civil examination,[2] and he asked the emperor to build a memorial archway to honor the chastity of his sister, who had remained unmarried to raise and support him. Another young woman was married to a widowed government official. At the death of her husband six months after the wedding, she was resolute to raise his four sons and to provide them with good educations. Because of her efforts, all of her husband's sons won official titles through civil service examinations. The emperor built another archway to honor her chastity. However, visitors to the temple could only see the woman's profile in her portrait. The official reason was that with a second-wife status, she was not eligible for a frontal portrait, despite her many sacrifices and contributions.

When I walked out of the temple, I felt depressed.

About eighty years have passed since the May Fourth movement against feudalism. Amidst applauses and praises for women's contributions, sacrifices, selflessness, and hard work, why don't we feel sympathy for them and outrage at the injustice? When we support women and encourage them to seek their own self-identity, why don't we ask men to make self-sacrifices as well?

I am not a feminist. On the scale of career and family, I seem to give more weight to the latter, according to my life situations and principles as a woman. I understand well what I have gained and what I have given up. I have decided to "waste" some time and miss some career opportunities after difficult internal debates. But I have never abandoned my own independence and self-respect as a woman.

Let us return to the news story. Of course, all well-written reports are not free of bias and errors. How can we, simply based on what we read from the newspaper, say that we know the innermost feelings of a woman who lived a complex life? When we applaud the woman for her hard work, generosity, and kindness, why don't we encourage her to seek and build her own happiness? Isn't this kind of support part of the nature-endowed duty and obligation of a husband, a son, or a brother?

It seems that the Chaste Temple in Anhui still casts a long historical shadow.

NOTES

1. *Lienü zhuan* compiled by Liu Xiang (79–8 B.C.E.) toward the end of the Former Han Dynasty (202 B.C.E.–C.E. 9) is the earliest book solely devoted to the moral education of women. An introduction by Anne Behnke Kinny is available at etext.lib.virginia.edu/chinese/lienu/browse/LienuIntro.html.

2. Held each year for bureaucratic recruitment from 100 B.C.E to 1905. Participants, exclusively male, were required to apply their knowledge of classical literature to prose-writing, or the eight-legged essay (*baguwen*).

GIVE HER SOME SPACE*

I was once labeled an "old miss" [*danü*]. At twenty-eight, I looked unlikely to marry.

As one of the earliest young hires at a factory during the Cultural Revolution, my single status became a main concern to my female coworkers, whose average age was forty-two. With combined efforts, they tried to rescue me from the plight of spinsterhood through overdosed friendship, nosy questions, and saucy teases. I, on the other hand, dealt with them tactically—sometimes with self-ridicule, sometimes with irony, sometimes with elusion, and sometimes with self-created fables. Incredibly, I won the upper hand at each encounter.

Later, younger employees aged between eighteen and twenty-two flocked to the factory. The girls were busy beautifying themselves, buzzing like bees to seek romance. Some of them wound up with happiness, but others were left sad, emotionally decreasing our productivity. Using me as a role model, the senior mentors advised them to concentrate on their jobs, but in the eyes of these young girls, I was only an aged spinster. The female protégés' attitudes in turn affected their mentors, who then turned around and looked at me with suspicion and sympathy, as if something were wrong with me.

In fact, I was secretly seeing my now husband who lived down the street. Our dating was disguised so well that nobody knew we were in a relationship. According to our island's custom, a girl who frequents her boyfriend's house would be frowned upon as a slut. So my husband came

---

*From the essay collection, *Sky-High Aspirations*, Shu Ting (Zhuhai, Guangdong: Zhuhai Press, 1994), 112–16.

to see me instead. At that time, I had just established my career and made friends with many writers who often visited me, particularly on weekends. While my friends spoke their minds freely and openly, my husband remained quiet, cleverly hiding his intelligence. Therefore, no one, except for my father, thought of us as a compatible couple.

At thirty-two, my husband was an "old bachelor" [*danan*], who, with his family background and good looks, must have rejected countless love letters and go-betweens' proposals.

Actually, our behaviors did not violate moral codes. I did not make our relationship public because once it was known, we would have to schedule a wedding date. I was happy with my single life and hoped to keep dating him forever. But along with my brother's marriage, his wife moved into our house. A kind woman, she took over duties that were originally mine—cooking, dishwashing, laundering, and cleaning. Although I was happy because I did not like housekeeping, I felt guilty for letting her take over all my obligations. I then tried to cover my guilt by attending as many writing seminars as possible. However, traveling was not a feasible solution to my life problems. Besides, my husband's parents, already seniors, dreamed daily about their youngest son being married.

At twenty-nine, I moved my possessions—books, manuscripts, and about twenty pots of roses—from the daughterly quarters to the wifely quarters.

Upon my husband's marriage proposal, we settled on three agreements. First, I would be free of domestic duties. Second, we would live as a nuclear family. Third, I would keep hanging out with my friends. But within a year of our marriage, all the agreements were broken. My in-laws moved in from Hong Kong to take care of our newborn. In a modern society, three generations living under the same roof counted as an extended family, not a nuclear one. A writer working from home most of the time, I naturally became responsible for all the housekeeping. Each morning, the alarm clock woke me up at six. I prepared breakfast for my son and organized his backpack for fear he might be late for school, while thinking about what soup to make for lunch and what food for supper. The laundry in the washer had yet to hang out to dry, my husband's socks had yet to be mended, the rooms had yet to be cleaned. When talking to visitors—interviewers or friends—about poetry, I fastened my heart to the clock on the wall. Its ticking reminded me of each passing second—I had to get the meal ready for my son's lunch break. Gradually, I had fewer visitors. Instead of visiting me, they called me. When the phone rang, I would quickly clean my hands on my apron and turn off the stove. Picking up the phone, I would burst out: "What's up? Sorry, got to go. The oil in my wok is sizzling."

Reading the essays of Jian Zhen, a Taiwanese female writer, I feel as if I were a swan flying freely over a fairyland. The pure soul and boundless mind reflected in her writing often makes me wonder what I have given up. I have decided that if anything happens to my marriage, I will never, ever, cage myself in marriage again.

However, there is no sign that my husband would leave me.

No way out. Because of my life experience, I relate passionately to each "old miss" in mainland China. Jian Zhen lives in economically advanced Taiwan where she enjoys a single life like a goddess, a life impossible for an ordinary mainland woman to attain. People in big cities—Beijing, Shanghai, and Guangzhou—are said to be liberal. The fast urban pace keeps them spinning around their own business without time to poke into their neighbors'. It is reported that some well-educated career "old misses" in Beijing would rather go out with married men on weekends than get married. I doubt if the news report is accurate, but I believe that this alternative lifestyle must have granted such women much freedom.

In the small town where I live, storms of well-intended inquiries and nosy gossips stalk single women, who are forced to give up their life plans eventually. A best friend of mine, tall and slender with beautiful eyes and personality, decided not to marry in order to enjoy a burden-free life. But her younger brother's marriage changed the structure of her space—she had to give up her room to the married couple and yield to a room too small to hold a twin bed. The limited space caused family rifts. For the sake of her mother, who was annoyed by the situation, my friend married upon a matchmaker's proposal. Her marriage changed her. She is silenced by a limited social life. Each time I see her cheerless, sick face, my heart cringes with pain.

As a single woman, I was stalked and interrogated when strolling along the beach. The stalker did not dispel the suspicion that I might be a defect sneaking across the gulf to Taiwan until I talked back in the local dialect and he saw my factory's safety gloves in my pockets. Immediately after the investigation, the person did not let me go but started to give me advice against "suicide," a presumption making me dumbfounded and speechless. Tired of the prolonged intrusion and lecture, I quit walking along the beach. Later, I found out the stalker was a volunteer coast guard on duty.

Indeed, a single woman causes suspicion in public—in movie theaters, parks, or restaurants. The ruthless spotlight in turn makes her doubt herself, her life.

British writer Virginia Woolf made a plea for a room of her own, a request each woman would second from the bottom of her heart. Yet her request, however simple and clear, has never been written into law.

A writer friend of mine, single and pretty with remarkable literary taste, has yet to meet the right man, despite her many great friendships. Day after day, year after year, amidst gossips and investigations, she has learned not to be bothered and tried to live a life of her own. Material reality, however, did not leave her alone. Her parents sighed heavily upon her return from work, because both her younger sister and brother had been married. She applied to her institute for a housing arrangement[1] but was told unmarried women were not eligible to apply. Finally, considering her seniority and her persistence, her institute granted her a small room in a new building. She was liberated, even though each time, at dawn or night, she had to dress decently before using the bathroom down the hall. Our society simply does not understand how important a private bathroom is to a woman. It is her sanctuary against interference and intrusion.

When institution-subsidized housing ownerships became available, my aforementioned friend applied to her institute but was told again single women were not eligible. She followed up with the question: "What if I remain single all my life?" No one could answer that question.

I hold strongly that a woman is unable to maintain her dignity and freedom unless she has her own income and residence. In a prosperous society, finding a job may not be too difficult. A woman will take a less desirable job when she does not have the best luck or the proper credentials. A room of her own, however, is too hard to obtain, no matter whether or not she is married.

As for a room to accommodate a woman's mind, perhaps no one can provide one.

NOTE

1. Until the late 1990s, most urban residents did not own houses. Institutes were responsible to allocate housing for their employees. In most cases, resources were limited. For these reasons, it was not rare to find three generations or extended families living together.

A MIRROR OF ONE'S OWN*

D o not let television impose on you the idea that you are a woman
writer, a writer of the female sex, because its screen is only a piece of
glass that never reflects you as accurately as a mirror.

Do not be a narcissist and admire your own sexy curves, because if a
woman constantly bats her long thick eyelashes, people think she suffers
from eye irritation.

Nowadays, the criteria for women's literature function like a net to
catch butterflies.

Those who want to be caught by the net would submissively fold their
colorful wings to be marked as samples, which, in consequence, would be
overstocked and sold cheaply by vendors. Those who have escaped the net
may be the most valuable because they are too active to be caught and too
different to attract the public's attention.

How many red cells are there in my blood? How much uric acid is
there in my body? Is there any early sign of cancer? These issues are my
doctor's business. I know I am in good health, so I travel, read in bed, eat
normal food, and occasionally drink a cup of coffee.

Is the context in which I write feminine or masculine? Are my feelings
as tough as steel cables or as flimsy as ants' antennae? Are my eyes normal
or crossed? Or are they too wide-set for my face? The critics who have
their own standards have their answers—fair answers (even if they are unfair
because of missing information, I do not mind). Regardless, I feel lucky to
be able to continue writing. As my son describes, I mail manuscripts in the

---

* The original appears in *Hong Kong Writer* 12 (1998): 2.

morning and receive royalty checks in the afternoon. In the evening, I call my friends to ask which seminar has sent me its invitation.

A woman having to disguise as a man in order to serve in the military is history. The story of *Hua Mulan* is indeed entertaining to young children. Now, we are told that if he uses a feminine pseudonym, a male writer may publish whatever he writes and receive critical acclaims. Is this a good sign, a sign for an age in which the female identity becomes as creditable as the credit card?

Hold your cheers.

The female-named writer seems to prove that it is easier to be a female writer than to be a male one. I want to point out, however, that the female writers whose names sound masculine testify otherwise. Xu Xiaobing, Chi Zijian, Xu Kun, and Cui Jianping are successful writers, in spite of their names. Their cases may instead lead to the conclusion that a male name helps a writer to establish a literary career. Then, how about changing the feminine first name of Bi Shumin to a masculine one? I do not think Bi would be happy.

Being a woman is hard. She must sustain her career advancement and deal with household finances and layoffs, while bearing exclusive domestic responsibilities, in addition to being her husband's companion and the child's educator.

Being a man is hard, too. Supposedly responsible for big national events, he must collect sufficient financial resources to save face on social occasions, while dealing with his wife's complaints at home.

The insect understands the gender situation and says to itself, "Being a human is hard. I had better keep my insect status to undergo a simply process—to hatch, to multiply, and to die."

Interestingly, no one uses men's literature as a special term.

Meanwhile, women's literature is often considered as being obsessed with career women, family matters, and women's issues. It is not even regarded as relevant as the literature on insects because the latter, at least, makes contributions to environmental protection.

All female characters in literature have been hitherto created by men. From this point of view, man serves not only as the rib for woman's creation but also as God.

In the second or third grade, I started reading *Dream of the Red Chamber* with an impressionable mind. Reading it again and again for more than ten

years, I have become more and more doubtful. Whenever someone
mends me on my Lin Daiyu–like personality, I am outraged because I
never liked her sentimentality, which makes other people uncomfortable.

Later, I started reading other literary canons and participated in the
discussions of "Nora" and "Anna Karenina." Gradually, I began to believe
in "God."

When can we eventually have our own mirror to reflect women's
literature and make it respectable?

125

com-
have

VII

ZHANG KANGKANG

Z hang Kangkang was born in 1950 in Hangzhou, Zhejiang Province. Zhang Kangkang is known as a leading figure of "wound literature," novels that depict the political persecution and hardship under Mao. Writing practically nonstop for over three decades, Zhang has published novels, novellas, short stories, memoirs, and numerous essays. Zhang now lives in Beijing as a professional writer. She is also the vice president of the Heilongjiang Writers' Association and a member of the Board of Directors of the China Writers' Association.

At the beginning of the Cultural Revolution, like other teenagers of her generation, Zhang threw herself into Mao Zedong's campaign to go to the poor and remote parts of rural China. For eight years, she worked on the Beidahuang Farm, a remote area in extreme poverty where Lu Xing'er also worked. As Zhang remembers:

> I left Hangzhou for the northeast at the age of nineteen during the Youth-Go-to-Countryside Campaign. Actually, I was quite willing to go there, for I was filled with youthful idealism. But the truth was that the life I'd hoped to embrace was quite tedious, and only in my mind could I keep a private domain. Like sometimes when I was busy working, I would think how to clean up some of my novel; sometimes, after I finished for the day, I would walk home and a light breeze would allow me to easily recall the scenes described in some Russian novels. At that time, literature served as a kind of spiritual encouragement for me. (quoted in "Female Writer")

In 1972, she debuted her short story "The Lamp," and in 1975 published her novel *The Borderline*. Her most renowned short story, "The Right to Love," was published in 1979 in *Shouhuo* [Harvest], one of China's most prestigious literary magazines. A year later, she published more short stories ("The Tolling of a Distant Bell," "The Egg's Philosophy," "Summer," "White Poppies," "The Dove Flying Away," and "Traveling Far") as well as a novel, *Northern Lights*. Her other works include *The Misty Morning Sun* (1980), *The Invisible Companion* (1986), *Reddish Red* (1995), *The Gallery of Romantic Love* (1996), *Woman on the Edge* (2002), which was adopted into a TV series, and many more. In addition, Zhang published many essay collections, such as *Say No to Your Fate*, *The Sea of Blue Waves*, and *The Dune*.

Zhang has received numerous literary awards as well, including the China Best Short Story Award for "Summer," the China Best Novelette Award for *The Misty Morning Sun*, the First Shanghai Literary Award for *The Red Poppies*, the Heilongjiang Province Fiction Contest Award for *The Invisible Companion*, the First Northeast China Essay Award for *A Collection of Zhang Kangkang's Essays*, the First Chinese Women's Literary Award, and others.

Zhang's essays are chosen from her collection *Say No to Your Fate*. Written gradually in a timespan of more than ten years, these three essays reflect the progression of Zhang's thinking about gender and women's writing. Of all the essays in this collection, Zhang's "We Need Two Worlds" is the most widely quoted essay by critics of Chinese women and literature, exactly because of her seemingly contradictory position on human issues versus women's issues. Indeed, readers may not fully appreciate Zhang when she says, "[w]hen there is no basic human equality, how could there be gender equality? For this reason, we cannot perceive society solely from a female standpoint." However, Zhang's position on gender politics cannot be separate from the sociocultural context out of which her writing has evolved. In "We Need Two Worlds," Zhang appeals for human values and dignity that were lost during the Cultural Revolution (Wu, "Alternative" 220–23). For example, her parents were politically persecuted in the 1950s and during the Cultural Revolution. She thinks that Mao's desexualization of women was rooted in the inhumanity of his administration and that women's problems are part of the human issues in China, where the government's agendas are held above human life. Under the same political circumstances, women writers struggle along with male writers for humanity and human rights.

Transcending male-female dualism, Zhang's concern symbolizes a gender-neutral feminism that asks for more than women's liberation. She envisions an ideal society where women and men live as equal human beings harmoniously with mutual respect, and that they play reciprocal and not separate roles (Wu, "Paradigm" 181). At the same time, she is aware that women writers "constantly fight against the condescension of their male colleagues and their own trivialization" (L. Liu 151). Therefore, she wants men to experience women's material lives through women's literature and to liberate themselves from patriarchal ideology, which systematically divides both sexes and suppresses women as a result.

To this end, Zhang believes that women writers bear additional responsibility to promote social awareness of humanity in order to educate men, to enhance women's self-confidence and self-esteem, and to improve women's lives, a belief that other writers in this collection share. But she feels that unless our society is truly equal, women would not be fully liberated. For example, in response to the question of whether she prefers to be a career woman or a good housewife, Zhang says:

> In an equal and sensible society, these two roles should not conflict. If there are good services, an advanced economy, and an equal pay system, women would be able to do both. But in today's society, women who want both are exhausted. As for myself, I am trying to do the best I can. (quoted in J. Wang)

Like Lu Xing'er's writing, Zhang's is also very much of her time. As Zhang's perspectives on gender have evolved, so has her writing. In "We Need Two Worlds," published in 1985, she decided to wait and prepare herself to produce "genuine" women's literature. Starting in the late 1990s, Zhang's transcendence of gender in "We Need Two Worlds" seems to give way to her attention to the characteristics of women's writing, a kind of writing that she esteems as more honest than men's in terms of truth and real life—for example, "The 'Grand' Realm versus the 'True' Realm" in this collection.

Her new perspective is exemplified by one of her novels, *Woman on the Edge* (2002). As Zhang comments:

> The term "woman on the edge" is not a notion. It is a phenomenon that represents many modern women and their ideals. My purpose of writing about this kind of women is to show how their behaviors go against the norm . . . *Woman on the Edge* questions women's positions defined by the centuries-long history and traditional culture. As a character, Zhuo'er's desire is not to collect material gains or change her fate as a woman, but to live a life true to her self, to enhance her spirits, and to fulfill her dreams. For this reason, she consistently tests herself through "self-challenges," a form of rebellion against oppressive tradition. Had she stopped being a woman on the edge, she would have not sent any progressive messages, and I would not have been inspired to write this novel. (quoted in Y. Li)

Woman on the Edge illustrates both Zhang's idea of "genuine" women's literature and her notion of the characteristics of female writing, a writing that grows from a woman's life experience that is unique to women and unknown to male writers. Like *Woman on the Edge*, Zhang's essays reflect her evolving feminist thinking under the specific sociopolitical circumstances that Chinese women, including herself, have been through under and after Mao.

Along with other writers in this collection, Zhang lets us witness a form of social engagement of both genders and a profound moment of history making in Chinese literary feminism, a feminism that evolves out of Chinese women's history, a feminism that embraces broader concerns of the humanity of equality through educating men and emancipating women from the "vicious cycles" of arguments over power, and a feminism unique to post–Mao Chinese women.

WE NEED TWO WORLDS*

SOCIETY IS SIMPLIFIED AND DISTORTED IF ONLY SEEN FROM A LIMITED FEMALE STANDPOINT

I am not familiar with the European definition of women's literature. Does it refer to literary works by women or all literary works about women's lives, including male works about women? If it merely stands for the former, then the definition of women's literature is too narrow, because this world is shared by both sexes. Male writers' presentations of women indispensably complement women's self-portraits. Tolstoy's *Anna Karenina* and *Resurrection*, German author [Heinrich] Boll's *The Unguarded House*, Austrian author [Stefan] Zweig's *Twenty Four Hours in the Life of a Woman*, and other excellent works all effectively describe women's everlasting miseries and pursuits. Therefore, I think women's literature inspires both sexes to experience women's love and hate.

My novels depict many female protagonists, but if they were replaced by males, the essential thoughts, emotions, and conflicts would still hold. This is because my writing centers on human issues, dealing with existential and spiritual crises faced by both sexes. The human issues, or issues about my country and my people, such as the destruction of humanity in the ten years of turmoil, the degradation of human dignity, the suppression of individuality, the censorship of ideas, as well as the spiritual emancipation and new values in the new era since 1978, have been my main concerns. They arrest more of my attention than women's future. Saying so, I do

---

* From Zhang's essay collection *Ni tui mingyun shuo bu* [Say No to Your Fate] (Shanghai: Knowledge Press, 1992), 260–66.

131

not mean to marginalize women's literature but rather to point out that, for many years to come, the sufferings shared by both sexes will remain a compelling central issue. Thus, women's liberation cannot be regarded as an isolated "women's issue." When there is no basic human equality, how could there be gender equality? For this reason, we cannot perceive society solely from a female standpoint. As a classical poem explains, once on the Lushan Mountain, one is unable to see its full image.[1] The limited view would be simplistic and biased.

For example, my works are popular among young people. After reading my novel, *Northern Lights*, a young man wrote to me that Cen Cen's persistence in pursuing her dream reflects his values. This instance proves that women's literary works also help male readers understand women's thoughtful, sensitive minds and, in turn, understand themselves as humans.

TRUE EQUALITY COMES FROM AN EQUAL CONCEPTUAL FRAMEWORK

Currently, an increasing number of educated women demand more freedom to express their academic ideas and to manage the state and institutions. They hope to be viewed as significant contributors and not simply as women in the traditional sense. They don't want their self-values to be assessed through their husbands; rather, they want their own individuality to come forth through their own work and social network. They want to speak their minds independently and act on their own to develop into full human beings and live a colorful life. They hold higher expectations of marriage than before, hoping to receive more affection and respect from their husbands. They also want to meet male friends to expand their social circles and to achieve self-enrichment and self-fulfillment. In a way, women try to adjust themselves between the past and the future to find a new position. However, their self-consciousness seems to have brought forth a series of problems. Divorce, separation, and single life as alternative lifestyles challenge the stable and peaceful traditional family structure, setting off rebellions against the persistently male-dominated society, which responds in panic. This may be a global trend. Repeatedly challenging the traditional mode of family, women bring new lives, new meanings, and new joys to romantic love, strengthening it continuously. In the past, Chinese women suffered silently in loveless marriages. Now they have broken the traditional shackles to live a life of love. Which lifestyle is more ethical? The answer, I think, is obvious. However, for the time being, I will not write fiction to address the controversy, nor will other women writers, because doing so means to squander away our valuable time on endless and fruitless arguments. In current China, the most sensitive writing is indeed women's literature and not exposé literature. However, in order to produce genuine women's literature, we have to wait and further prepare ourselves.

This is unfortunate to contemporary women.

In a backward and uneducated society, women's liberation unfortunately encounters stubborn resistance from women themselves, because tradition has its deep roots in their minds.

Undoubtedly, history, nature, and society have been unfair to women. The injustices are committed not only through traditional ideologies, such as "male superiority and female inferiority" and male chauvinism, but also through the erosion of women's willpower. Thousands of years of feudal oppression, inherited ideologies, and the survival of a hard life—all these "natural laws" have deprived women of the strong will that is fundamental to independence and self-esteem. They are unable to free themselves from dependency and habitude. They are more interested in the family, the husband, and the child than in their own personal development. Men then turn women's sacrifices into reasons to look down upon them. It is in this vicious cycle that women are crawling. Therefore, if we want to motivate women to change their lives, merely criticizing the male in our writing does not suffice. Women writers must gather courage to face ourselves, focus on women, and educate and improve them (including ourselves) to overcome deep-rooted weaknesses, such as vanity, dependency, jealousy, pettiness, narrow-mindedness, etc. Only when we enhance our self-value through our achievements can we forcefully battle male egocentricity, selfishness, arrogance, brutality, and callousness and finally win men's respect.

The significance of women's literature resides in developing women's consciousness. This development is a long, challenging process.

Let me give an example. A group of co-ed college students was engaged in a heated debate. A female student accused the male students, "You guys don't act like men; why don't you just let us win?" This is the mentality of "the frail woman"[2] who does not have sufficient self-esteem and whose success depends on her rival's mercy. The equity achieved through this mental inequality is not true equality, because it is similar to accepting chivalrous protection. Regardless, some women still want "male patronage" without realizing that pleading for mercy devalues their selfhood. And devalued womanhood is exactly what the traditional society wants. From this viewpoint, the most oppressive force may not be social contempt for women but their own perception of themselves as perfectly frail women.

It is hard to say whether men or women are better because both have their own issues and, meanwhile, share some common problems. Thus, we cannot view male and female as absolute opposites, because in real life tensions within the same sex are often more fierce than those between the sexes.

Therefore, we need two worlds.

OUR PHYSIOLOGICAL DISADVANTAGE IS GOD'S FAULT; OUR POTENTIAL COMES FROM HARD WORK AND SELF-EMPOWERMENT

In the 1970s, Chinese women were suddenly elevated to a "noble" and "paramount" position. Numerous female oil workers, firefighters, and miners were born. Female characters in literature were masculinized with exaggerated heavy facial features of thick eyebrows and big eyes. Militant in the "revolutionary spirit" and apathetic to romantic love, they preferred army uniforms to dresses. However, the revolutionary image supposedly symbolizing women's liberation only signifies an unforgivable historic setback, because it does not reflect the true human nature. Women were virtually killed when deprived of the right to be beautiful, exquisite, and elegant. During this long era, the female was virtually nonexistent in China. This is a serious traumatic lesson. Now women live in a modern age with higher respect for womanhood. While they may not want to do whatever men do physically, they want to have the same confidence and ability as men to do what they deem suitable for themselves. In other words, they do not want to be the same as men; rather, they want to remain women who are different from men and have more charisma than men. They want careers, successes, and honors, as well as romantic love, children, and friendships. Women have started to fight back, even though long-lasting traditional morals and conventions hold steadfast.

Inevitably, there are new challenges because work and family often conflict. For instance, it is hard for diligent professional women to find spouses because men only want virtuous wives and good mothers to serve them at home. Meanwhile, under the double burden of family and work, the intelligence and tenacity sustaining middle-aged[3] women's accomplishments and competitive edge may give way to physiological constraints. This injustice to our body is God's fault. What we can do is overcome the disadvantage through hard work and perseverance. When convinced by our potentials, men will eventually have to acknowledge, not as a lip service but from the bottom of their hearts, that women deserve the right to manage the same world. In China, it is particularly important to modernize the concept of woman. Otherwise, true modernization is impossible to achieve.

Only when men do not need Women's Day to remind them to respect women, can women truly celebrate their own holiday.

NOTES

1. From a poem by Su Shi ([Su Dongpo] 1037–1101), a leading literary figure in the Song Dynasty. The Lushan Mountain is a summer resort in Jiangxi Province in South China. The original lines—"I cannot see the whole image of Lushan Mountain / Only because I am in the mountain"—are often used to refer to a narrow or provincial view.

2. Borrowed from Shakespeare—"Frailty, thy name is woman"—"frail woman" (*ruo nüzi*) was first used by Yutang Lin in his essays to refer to women's dependence on men for life and protection. Now this term is often used in contrast to man.

3. Women of thirty-five or older and men of forty years or older are considered middle-aged.

A PREFACE FOR MYSELF*

I t is hard not to write essays, because they are not only natural and unpretentious but also truthful, a quality most appealing to me.

I often feel that fiction writers work like weavers who shuttle threads on looms to fabricate an imaginary reality day in and day out, replacing others' imaginations with their own and satisfying their desires with fiction. Sometimes I become tired of fiction writing, for it would be needless if we could still use tree leaves as clothing. On the other hand, I feel that writing fiction is like building a bridge for readers to cross. It is also like making a boat, which the writer steers with a bamboo pole to ferry readers across the river. The bridge must not collapse; the boat must not leak. Once on the other bank, you are supposed to hide behind a tree and watch as your passengers take different directions. Their destinations are their own decisions.

I am concerned about my own destination.

Knowing there is no heaven or hell, I wander in this world, supposedly to follow the footprints of prior generations. These random, endless footprints fill me with fear—a fear of being lost on this vast land.

Trekking alone on the noiseless plain under the expansive sky, I only hear my lonesome murmurs. In an internal dialogue, my mind is confiding to my soul.

Human beings need to converse not only with others but also with themselves.

From this viewpoint, fiction is written for others, while essays for writers themselves.

---

* An excerpt from "Preface to the *Collection of Authorized Essays*" in *Canglang zhi shui* [The Sea of Blue Waves], Zhang Kangkang (Nanjing, Jiangsu: Jiangsu Arts and Literature Press, 1998), 177–79.

This is when the essay is born.

When an essay flows from the tip of the pen, I feel as if I inhaled clean air. Being cleansed, my heart quivers in thrill.

I am aware that I am often brusque and impatient.

As such, I often stop weaving to go to the woods, looking for the single genuine rope amongst dead grass and dry tree branches. I do not take the bridge or the ferryboat. Nor do I want to build them. Instead, I take off my heavy, burdensome clothes by the bank of the racing river and plunge into the clear, warm water, letting it wave through my hair, cleanse me, and caress my body.

I hope and also believe that other swimmers will walk with me into the water. Needing no boat or bridge, we go either along the stream or against it candidly without worry.

This is when the essay is born.

The essay serves as a loyal companion.

Its loyalty grows out of one's honesty, rewarding one with heart-to-heart companionship. Experiencing all sorts of human emotions, be they sorrow, grief, happiness, or excitement, I look for a river where I can let my mind go.

My essays show my identity more than my fiction does. If fiction reflects the truth by revealing the nature of life, then the essay is the transparent truth itself.

The essay is said to be the most beautiful genre. A truly beautiful essay, however, must be written on blank paper without dissemblance.

THE "GRAND" REALM VERSUS THE "TRUE" REALM*

I do not believe all essays written by females can be called women's (*nüxing*) essays. In fact, for a long time, women's essays hardly existed in China.

During that time, one was not allowed to be a woman (*nüren*).[1] How could there be any women's essays?

Women's (*nüxing*) minds, women's emotional expressions, women's worldviews, women's lifestyles, women's intellectual pursuits, and women's self-reflections—these are essential components of women's essays.

The essay of the Chinese woman (*nüxing*) waited for her moment in the early 1980s and, in the 1990s, finally seized her opportunity with the rhetoric of "returning to femininity" to unveil her long-concealed, suppressed visage in numerous rapidly growing evening newspapers and weekend columns.

Unfortunately, daily responsibilities, family disputes, conjugal matters, and children's education make life inevitably mundane. Women (*nüren*), in their seemingly prosaic yet refined, hearty language, analyze life and tell about the tough survivals of career women, the perplexity posed by marriage and romantic love, and the desire for beauty and compassion. . . . Using the pen, they blend together all sorts of insights and life experiences, and using paper as plates, they cater feasts of writing to readers.

Vividly narrating what happens between women, between women and men, between other women and themselves, women write, little by little and piece by piece, to strengthen one another. They hope that amidst women's care and solace, the dust of war will settle, men's noises will die down, and peaceful life will return.

---

* Selected from Zhang's essay collection, *Cang lang zhi shui* [The Sea of Blue Waves] (Nanjing: Jiangsu Arts and Literature Press, 1998), 25–26.

Suppose the world had only oceans but no rivers, only storms but no clear moonlit nights, only yelling but no smiles, only woods but no flowers—for what, then, do we live?

In her essay, the woman searches for her identity and her soul. Crossing the bridge of words, she dispels anxieties and cultivates her intellect to reach the spiritual realm of her heart.

The grand realm does not have to be explored through big events. Nor does it stand for empty, belligerent words. All subtle, ordinary, and trivial life details inspire grandeur. In fact, the spirit of equality, freedom, and love is embedded in daily routines that many of us overlook.

From an extremely ordinary life, women have developed their personal philosophies that may reveal more truths than those developed from "important affairs" in the male world of power struggles and political conspiracies. In such a patriarchal society abound with competition, deception, greed, and violence, where can we find inspiration of grandeur? The supposedly grand male realm of important affairs merely creates myths and illusions that not only make men superficial and hypocritical but also change women back into the means for men's ambitions.

Women's essays do not have to embrace "the grand realm," but should explore "the true realm."

NOTES

1. See "Translator's Note" for woman naming.

SUPPLEMENTAL READINGS

Bi, Shumin. "Broken Transformers." *Chinese Literature* (Summer 1992): 88–98.

———. "The Hitchhiker." *Chinese Literature* (Spring 1997): 47–58.

———. "An Appointment with Death." *Chinese Literature* (Spring 1997): 5–45.

Contemporary Chinese Women Writers: Three Novellas by Fang Fang. Volume V. Beijing: China Books & Periodicals, 1996.

Fang Fang. "Landscape." *Contemporary Chinese Women Writers.* Volume II. Beijing: Panda Books, 1991 (18–135).

Hu, Xin. "Four Women of Forty." In *The Serenity of Whiteness: Stories by and About Women in Contemporary China*, edited and translated by Zhu Hong. New York: Ballantine Books, 1991 (158–87).

Lu, Xing'er. "Under One Roof." *Chinese Literature* (Winter 1990): 45–59.

———. "The Sun Is Not Out Today." In *The Serenity of Whiteness: Stories By and About Women in Contemporary China*, edited and translated by Zhu Hong. New York: Ballantine Books, 1991 (188–207).

———. "The One and the Other." In *The Serenity of Whiteness: Stories By and About Women in Contemporary China*, edited and translated by Zhu Hong. New York: Ballantine Books, 1991 (208–26).

Shu, Ting. "Poems." In *Contemporary Chinese Literature: An Anthology of Post-Mao Fiction and Poetry,* edited by Michael Duke. New York: M.E. Sharpe, 1984 (52–54).

———. "The Wall." In *Seeds of Fire: Chinese Voices of Conscience*, edited by Geremie Barmé and John Minford. New York: Hill and Wang, 1988. 18.

———. "Memories." In *Anthology of Modern Chinese Poetry*, edited and translated by Michelle Yeh. New Haven, Conn.: Yale University Press, 1992 (184–85).

———. "Dedication." In *Anthology of Modern Chinese Poetry*, edited and translated by Michelle Yeh. New Haven, Conn.: Yale University Press, 1992 (185–86).

———. "Assembling Line." In *Anthology of Modern Chinese Poetry*, edited and translated by Michelle Yeh. New Haven, Conn.: Yale University Press, 1992 (186).

———. "Goddess Peak." In *Anthology of Modern Chinese Poetry*, edited and translated by Michelle Yeh. New Haven, Conn.: Yale University Press, 1992 (186–87).

————. *Selected Poems: An Authorized Collection*, translated by Eva Hung. Hong Kong: Research Center for Transaction, Chinese University of Hong Kong Press, 1994.

————. *Shu Ting: Selected Poems*. Renditons Press, 1994.

————. "A Performing Style." *Chinese Literature*. (Spring 1994): 151–52.

————. "Untitled." *Chinese Literature*. (Autumn 1995): 166–67.

————. *Mist of My Heart: Selected Poems of Shu Ting*, translated by Gordon Osing. Beijing: Chinese Literature, 1995.

Zhang, Kangkang. "The Wasted Years." In *Seven Contemporary Chinese Women Writers*. Beijing: Panda Books, 1982 (237–55).

————. "Northern Lights," translated by Daniel Bryant. *Chinese Literaure* (Winter 1988): 92–102.

————. "The Right to Love." In *One Half of the Sky*, translated by R. A. Roberts and Angela Knox. New York: Dodd, Mead and Company, 1988 (51–81).

————. "The Spirit of Fire." In *The Rose Colored Dinner*, translated by Nienling Liu. Hong Kong: Joint Publishing, 1988 (51–79).

Zhang, Kangkang, and Mei Jin. "The Tolling of a Distant Bell." In *Contemporary Chinese Literature: An Anthology of Post-Mao Fiction and Poetry*, edited by Michael Duke. New York: M.E. Sharpe, 1984 (98–105).

BIBLIOGRAPHY

Ai, Xiaoming. "Women's Issues in China: Some Facts." *ASIANetwork: Exchange* VIII, no. 1 (Fall 2000): 17–19.

Apodaca, Clair. "The Effects of Foreign Aid on Women's Attainment of Their Economic and Social Human Rights." *Journal of Third World Studies* 17, no. 2 (2000): 202–27.

Barlow, Tani. "Politics and Protocols of *Funü*: (Un)Making National Woman." In *Engendering China: Women, Culture, and the State*, edited by Christina Gilmartin, Gail Hershatter, Lisa Rofel, and Tyrene White. Cambridge, Mass.: Harvard University Press, 1994 (339–59).

———. *The Question of Women in Chinese Feminism*. Durham, N.C.: Duke University Press, 2004.

Barlow, Tani, and Gary Bjorge, eds. *I Myself Am a Woman: Selected Writings of Ding Ling*. Boston: Beacon Press, 1989.

de Beauvoir, Simone. *The Second Sex*, translated by H. M. Parshley. New York: Alfred A. Knopf, 1971.

Bi, Shumin. *Tixing xingfu* (The Reminder of Happiness). Zhuhai, Guangzhou: Zhuhai Press, 1996.

"Bi Shumin." zt.tibet.cn/zt/zt2002003725152327.html (accessed July 23 2009).

Bufffton, Deborah. "Finding Their Voices: Stages of Liberation in the Works of Chinese Women Writers Since 1920." *MIFLC-Review* 1 (1991): 35–45.

Chang, Kang-I Sun, and Haun Saussy, eds. *Women Writers of Traditional China: An Anthology of Poetry and Criticism*. Stanford, Calif.: Stanford University Press, 1999.

Chen, Mingxia. "The Marriage Law and the Rights of Chinese Women in Marriage and the Family." *Holding up Half the Sky*, edited by Tao Jie, Zheng Bijun, and Shirley L. Mow. New York: Feminist Press, 2004 (159–71).

Chow, Ray. "Violence in the Other Country: China as Crisis, Spectacle, and Woman." In *Third World Women and the Politics of Feminism*, edited by Chandra T. Mohanty, Ann Russo, and Lourdes Torres. Bloomington: Indiana University Press, 1991 (81–100).

Croll, Elizabeth. *Changing Identities of Chinese Women*. London: Zed Books, 1995.

Dooling, Amy, and Kristina Torgeson, eds. *Writing Women in Modern China: An Anthology of Women's Literature from the Early Twentieth Century*. New York: Columbia University Press, 1998.

"*Duocai de nüxing huajuan*" [Colorful Portraits of Women]. *Wenhui dushu zhoubao* [Wenhui Reader's Weekly] (March 25, 1989): 2.

Engels, Frederick. *The Origin of Family, Private Property and the State*. New York: Pathfinder, 1972.

Fan, Carol. "Feminist Movements in China." *Literary Studies East and West* 12 (1996): 15–27.

Fang, Fang. *Chumen kan fengjing* [Go Sightseeing]. Xi'an, Shanxi: Shanxi shifan daxue chuban she [Shanxi Teachers' University Press], 1998.

———. "Speech at Central China University of Science and Technology." news.hustonline.net/Html/2006-4-22/29026.shtml (accessed July 23, 2008).

"Female Writer Zhang Kangkang." www.china.org.cn/english/NM-e/87835.htm (accessed August 29, 2008).

Han, Xiohui. *Nüren buhui ku* [Women Don't Cry]. Beijing: Huaqiao chubanshe [Overseas Chinese Press], 1998.

Hershatter, Gail. *Women in China's Long Twentieth Century*. Berkeley: University of California Press, 2007.

Honig, Emily, and Gail Hershatter. *Personal Voices: Chinese Women in the 1980s*. Stanford, Calif.: Stanford University Press, 1988.

Hu, Xin. "Four Women of Forty." In *The Serenity of Whiteness: Stories By and About Women in Contemporary China*, edited and translated by Zhu Hong. New York: Ballantine Books, 1991 (158–87).

———. *Nüren de yanjing* [Women's Eyes]. Nanchang: Baihuazhou wenyi chubanshe [Baihuazhou Arts and Literature Press], 1998.

Hu, Shih. "*Nüren yeshi ren*" [Women Are Also Humans]. In *Mingren tan nüren* [Renowned Writers on Women]. Haikou, Hainan: Hainan Press, 1992 (42–43).

Jia, Pingwa. *Shuohua* [Speaking]. Xi'an, Shaanxi: People's Press, 1995.

Jiang, Yongping. "Employment and Chinese Urban Women Under Two Systems." In *Holding Up Half the Sky*, edited by Tao Jie, Zheng Bijun, and Shirley Mow. New York: Feminist Press, 2004 (207–20).

Legge, James, trans. *Li Chi: Book of Rites*. New Hyde Park, N.Y.: University Books, 1967.

Li, Sangyin. "The Patterned Lute." www.dpo.uab.edu/~yangzw/lishy1.html#1.2 (accessed August 26, 2007).

Li, Xiaojiang. "Economic Reform and the Awakening of Chinese Women's Collective Consciousness." In *Engendering China: Women, Culture, and the State*, edited by Christina Gilmartin, Gail Hershatter, Lisa Rofel, and Tyrene White. Cambridge, Mass.: Harvard University Press, 1994 (360–82).

Li, Yan. "Zhang Kangkang." news.xinhuanet.com/book/2004-08/17/content_1804409.htm (accessed July 23, 2007).

Liang Shiqiu. *"Nüren"* [Woman]. In *Mingren tan nüren* [Renowned Writers on Women]. Haikou, Hainan: Hainan Press, 1992 (37–41).

Lin, Julia, trans. *Women of the Red Plain: An Anthology of Contemporary Chinese Women's Poetry*. New York: Penguin Books, 1993.

Lin, Yutang. *My Country and My People*. New York: John Day, 1939.

Liu, Lydia H. "Invention and Intervention: The Making of a Female Tradition in Modern Chinese Literature." In *Chinese Femininities/Chinese Masculinities: A Reader*, edited by Susan Brownell and Jeffrey N. Wasserstrom. Berkeley: University of California Press, 2002 (149–74).

Liu, Shih Shun. *Chinese Classical Prose: The Eight Masters of the Tang-Sung Period*. Hong Kong: Chinese University Press, 1979.

Lu, Qingfei, ed. *Dangdai qingnian nuzuojia pingzhuan* [The Biographical Commentary on Contemporary Women Writers]. Beijing: China Women's Press, 1990.

Lu, Tonglin. "Introduction." In *Gender and Sexuality in Twentieth-Century Chinese Literature and Society*, edited by Tonglin Lu. Albany: State University of New York Press, 1993 (1–22).

Lu, Xing'er. "The Sun is Not Out Today." In *The Serenity of Whiteness: Stories By and About Women in Contemporary China*, edited and translated by Zhu Hong. New York: Ballantine Books, 1991 (188–207).

———. *Nüren bu tiansheng* [One is Not Born Woman]. Shanghai: Shanghai chudian [Shanghai Bookstore Press], 1996.

Ma, Fengzao, and An Dongliang, eds. *Jianming xiezuo jiaocheng* [A Sourcebook for the Writing Course]. Tianjing: Nankai University Press, 1998.

———. "Qi Jue: Militia Women Inscription on a Photograph." www.xys.org/xys/ebooks/literature/poetry/Mao_poetry/mao3.txt (accessed July 23, 2007).

———. "Shui Diao Ge Tou: Re-Ascending the Jinggang Mountain." www.xys.org/xys/ebooks/literature/poetry/Mao_poetry/mao3.txt (accessed July 23, 2007).

———. "The Foolish Old Man Who Removed the Mountains." *Selected Works by Mao Zedong*. Volume III. art-bin.com/art/omao21.html (accessed July 23, 2007).

———. "A Reply to Li Shuyi." chineseculture.about.com/library/literature/poetry/blsmao_e24.htm.

McDougall, Bonnie S., and Kam Louie. *The Literature of China in the Twentieth Century*. New York: Columbia University Press, 1997.

Min, Dongchao. "From Asexualilty to Gender Differences in Modern China." In *Mary Wollstonecraft and 200 Years of Feminisms*, edited by Eileen Janes Yeo. New York: Rivers Oram, 1997 (193–203).

Okin, Susan Moller. "Feminism, Women's Human Rights, and Cultural Differences." *Hypatia* 13, no. 2 (Spring 1998): 32–52.

Pollard, David. *The Chinese Essay*. New York: Columbia University Press, 2000.

Riddell-Dixon, Elizabeth. "Mainstreaming Women's Rights: Problems and Prospects Within the Center for Human Rights." *Global Governance* 5 (1999): 149–71.

Rofel, Lisa. "Liberation Nostalgia and a Yearning for Modernity." In *Engendering China: Women, Culture, and the State*, edited by Christina Gilmartin, Gail Hershatter, Lisa Rofel, and Tyrene White. Cambridge, Mass.: Harvard University Press, 1994 (226–49).

Shu, Ting. *Ying gu ling xiao* [Sky-High Aspirations]. Zhuhai: Zhuhai Press, 1994.

Stacey, Judith. *Patriarchy and Socialist Revolution in China*. Berkeley: University of California Press, 1983.

Waley, Arthur, trans. *The Book of Songs*. New York: Grove/Atlantic, 1996.

Wang, Jun. "*Zhang Kangkang lun chuangzuo*" [Zhang Kangkang on Writing]. *Chinese Women's Daily*. December 1, 2003. oh100.pc163.com.cn/art/wenxue/eye/accessing/200312/0107040702296.html (accessed July 23, 2007).

Wang, Zheng. "Three Interviews." In *Gender Politics in Modern China: Writing and Feminism*, edited by Tani Barlow. Durham, N.C.: Duke University Press, 1993 (158–208).

———. "Maoism, Feminism, and the UN Conference on Women: Women's Studies Research in Contemporary China." *Journal of Women's History* 8, no. 4 (1997): 126–52.

Wu, Hui. "The Alternative Feminist Discourse of Post-Mao Chinese Writers." In *Alternative Rhetorics: Challenges to the Rhetorical Tradition*, edited by Laura Gray-Rosendale and Sibylle Gruber. Albany: State University of New York Press, 2001 (219–34).

———. "The Paradigm of Margaret Cavendish: Reading Women's Alternative Rhetorics in a Global Context." In *Calling Cards: Theory and Practice in the Study of Race, Gender, and Culture*, edited by Jacqueline Jones Royster and Ann Marie Mann Simpkins. Albany: State University of New York Press, 2005 (171–86).

Xie, Mian. "*Sanwen de jingsui shi ziyou*" [Freedom is the Essay's Essence]. *Jianming xiezuo jiaocheng* [A Sourcebook for the Writing Course], edited by Ma Fengzao and An Dongliang. Tianjing: Nankai University Press, 1998.

Xinmin Evening News [*Xinmin wanbao*]. 19 May (1998): 27.

Xiong, Yu. "The Status of Chinese Women in Marriage and the Family." In *Holding Up Half the Sky*, edited by Tao Jie, Zheng Bijun, and Shirley Mow. New York: Feminist Press, 2004 (172–78).

Zhang, Kangkang. "The Right to Love." In *One Half of the Sky: Stories from Contemporary Women Writers of China*, edited and translated by R. A. Roberts and Angela Knox. New York: Dodd, Mead and Company, 1988 (51–88).

———. *Ni tui mingyun shuo bu* [Say No to Your Fate]. Shanghai: Shanghai zhishi chubanshe [Shanghai Knowledge Press], 1992.

———. *canglang zhi shui* [The Sea of Blue Waves]. Nanjing, Jiangsu: Jiangsu weyi chubanshe [Jiangsu Arts and Literature Press], 1998.

———. *Zuo nü* [Woman on the Edge]. Beijing: Huayi chubanshe [China Arts Press], 2002.

Zhong, Xueping, Wang Zheng, and Bai Di, eds. *Some of Us: Chinese Women Growing Up in the Mao Era*. Brunswick, N.J.: Rutgers University Press, 2001.

Zhu, Ziqing. "*Nüren*" [Woman]. *Mingren tan nüren* [Renowned Writers on Women]. Haikou, Hainan: Hainan Press, 1992 (72–78).

PRIMARY SOURCES IN CHINESE

Han, Xiaohui. *Huiluo, huiluo* [Bribery, Bribery]. Shenyang, Liaoning: Liaoning renmin chubanshe [Liaoning People's Press], 1990.

———. *You hua dui ni shuo* [Something to Say to You]. Beijing: Qunzhong chubanshe [Populace Press], 1994.

———. *Buchu zhaozedi* [Out of Swamps]. Xi'an: Shaanxi renmin chubanshe [Shaanxi People's Press], 1994.

———. *Zichao* [Self-Ridicule]. Chongqing, Sichuan: Wenyi chubanshe [Sichuan Arts and Literature Press], 1994.

———. *Youyou xin hui* [Heart to Heart]. Beijing: Zhongguo wenlian chubanshe [China Association for Arts and Literature Press], 1995.

———. *Tiyan zibei* [Experiencing Embarrassment]. Shanghai: Dongfang zhongxin chubanshe [East Central Press], 1997.

———. *Nüren buhui ku* [Women Don't Cry]. Beijing: Haiwai chubanshe [China Overseas Press], 1998.

———. *Han xiaohui sanwen* [Essays of Han Xiaohui]. Fuzhou, Fujian: Huaxia chubanshe [Huaxia Press], 1999.

———. *Xihuan fu jingjie* [The Happy Buddhist]. Beijing: Xiandao chubanshe [Modern Press], 1999.

Lu, Xing'er. *Nüren bu tiansheng* [Women Are Not Born]. Shanghai: Shanghai Bookstore Press, 1996.

Hu, Xin. *Nüren de yanjing* [Women's Eyes]. Nanchang: Baihuazhou wenyi chubanshe [Baihuazhou Arts and Literature Press], 1998.

Shu, Ting. *Ying gu ling xiao* [Sky-High Aspirations]. Zhuhai: Zhuhai Press, 1994.

———. *Collection of Shu Ting's Essays*. Zhuhai: Zhuhai Press, 1994.

INDEX